Great Chicago Stories

Portraits and Stories

Great Chicago Stories

Portraits and Stories

TOM MADAY & SAM LANDERS

Seventy-first and Jeffrey, Copyright © David Mamet, 1994
Thoughts for My Daughter, Copyright © Anchee Min
No Place for a Poet, Copyright © Ana Castillo
The Naked City, Copyright © Sara Paretsky

Chicago, excerpted with permission from *Chicago*
(Pantheon Books, 1985-6) Copyright © Studs Terkel, 1994

First Edition

ISBN (North America) 0-9641703-0-2

Library of Congress Catalog Card Number 94-060776

Published by TwoPress Publishing Co., Chicago
Printed in Japan

For Kathy & Gerry

Contents

Contents

Great
Chicago
Stories

Portraits and Stories

a

Foreword

Clichés about big cities make me very uneasy. *If you can make it in New York, you can make it anywhere. I lost my heart in San Francisco. Aren't the traffic, earthquakes, mudslides, riots and smog awful in L.A.? People in Chicago have their feet on the ground.* There is usually just enough truth in clichés that they provide a spark of recognition, but somehow I feel guilty when I'm expected to nod my head in easy affirmation of them. And I find it difficult to gush, "I love Chicago" as a simple declaration.

My affection for Chicago is complex, miscellaneous, ambivalent, deep, skeptical, naive and ever-changing. My emotional connection to Chicago resides in the particulars: wolfing down a five-dollar meal of baked ham, biscuits and coleslaw among working men and women at Valois in Hyde Park, hitting a soaring tee shot down the fairway of the first hole at Waveland, the fear and trembling of driving up Lake Shore Drive in a blinding snowstorm, the memories of buying a used tennis racket at the Maxwell Street Market, nervously conducting the first interview I ever had with Nelson Algren, lying on a blanket and listening to music at a Grant Park summer concert, walking down Wabash Avenue and hearing the sounds of jazz burst into counterpoint against the screech of the overhead El, witnessing the brilliance of the Loop sky-line on a clear autumn evening, sparring in press conferences with the late Richard J. Daley, recalling the ubiquitous tear gas at the 1968 Democratic National Convention, recoiling at the memory of ninety-two students and three nuns killed in the Our Lady of the Angels School fire of 1958, and a million other sad, funny, dear, memorable images of life in Chicago.

Some of the stories you are about to read remind me of my own. Oprah Winfrey flew here for an audition in 1983. She recalls, "...as I landed at O'Hare, I had this strange feeling that I was coming home and that this was the place where I would live and build my life." I experienced an identical sense of homecoming and belonging when I arrived in Chicago with 71 cents in my pocket one cold February day in 1956. As I trudged up out of the Randolph Street IC Station and shivered as I walked west, I felt an odd elation. I was somehow filled with a realization that I had chosen the right city and that I would "make it" in Chicago, even though I didn't know a single soul in this city at the time.

Mirroring the experiences of several of the storytellers in this book (bluesman Buddy Guy down to his last dime, Sophie Madej of Sophie's Busy Bee restaurant without a dime to buy food), I had help at every step of my Chicago journey, much of it at precisely the time I needed it the most and from people who didn't have much themselves. Who would ever think that a hardened job placer at a down-scale Loop employment agency would take pity on me and lend me ten dollars out of his own wallet (a considerable sum in 1956) and see to it that I received vouchers that would enable me to live at the YMCA Hotel on South Wabash Avenue? In order to receive the vouchers I had to walk all the way down to the 12th Street Station and submit to an interview by a caseworker for Traveler's Aid. This engaging but no-nonsense black woman listened patiently as I explained that I had dropped out of college and had come to Chicago hoping to make enough money to return to school in a year or so. She asked me if my parents knew where I was. It was the question I hoped she wouldn't ask. Two months earlier I had experienced a terrible fight with my mother at home during Christmas break and it wouldn't be too great a leap to suggest that not only was I dropping out of college but also I was running away from home (I was 19 years old). I looked her in the eye and told her that my parents did not know where I was but that I planned to write to them the minute I was able to check into the Y Hotel. Did I want to call them, she asked? No, that's okay, I'll write, I said. She looked long and hard at me and said, "Okay, I'll take a chance on you." She gave me the room and food vouchers and also gave me some needed advice on how to obtain a checking account as soon as possible. Thank God she didn't send me home.

And just as George Wendt reports in this book that one of the most valuable learning experiences he ever had at *Second City* was getting booed off the stage, I am forever grateful to the poor but wise director at the YMCA theater group who informed me that I was the worst actor he had ever worked with and would I please do the American theater and myself a great favor and choose another line of work, perhaps journalism. Thank you, sir, wherever you are.

The power of this volume is found in the *details* of the stories and portraits, and in the widely diverse voices of the storytellers. Oh, there are some generalizations, but they are supported by enticing narratives. Comedian Tim Kazurinsky refers to his "abiding affection for this big, dopey city" and displays it with the recollection of a sweet, slightly wacky scene outside Marshall Field's at Christmas. Novelist Richard Stern explicitly shouts his love for Chicago, but only after treating us to one of his incomparably poignant essays. David Mamet doesn't explicitly proclaim his love for Chicago but displays it in the rendering of his chocolate phosphate-drinking, cartoon-watching, fist-fighting days and nights in the 71st Street Jewish neighborhood of his youth. And then there's Judge Abraham Lincoln Marovitz's unforgettable and hilarious story of how his mother came to name him Abraham Lincoln.

The venerable Studs Terkel, in the concluding chapter of this book, reminds us that Nelson Algren got it right when he spoke of the "doubleness" of Chicago—a Chicago for winners, a Chicago for losers. We need to remind ourselves that this book contains the stories of the winners. There are no stories here from young victims of drive-by shootings, or drug-addicted prostitutes, or angry old people who have given up hope because they were given none. The stories you will read in this volume are from Chicagoans who were given, and took, a chance—and made the most of it. And, thank God, most, if not all of them are what Algren referred to as "Go-Getters," not selfish "Go-Get-It-Yourselfers." They are people who are trying to make this city free of the conditions that give rise to the harsher realities of life in Chicago. They are people who have not given up on this city.

If Chicago is no longer Sandburg's city of Stockyards and Broad Shoulders, then it's the city of international futures trading and global communication. And even if Chicago is no longer perceived as the great literary capital it once was, several of the storytellers in these pages are part of the nation's greatest theater community. And even if Chicago is still the most racially segregated city in America, there are among our contributors the people who will work till their deaths to undo the pain and suffering of racism.

The complexity of life in Chicago today defies simple characterizations. But for me what powerfully represents the link between Chicago's past and its present is that however cold and windy, however cruel and heartless, this city continues to welcome strangers to its streets. That stranger can be a nearly penniless boy from West Virginia in 1956, or it can be a young painter from China who escapes Mao's Cultural Revolution and arrives here not speaking a word of English but is accepted into the School of the Art Institute. The story of Anchee Min contained in this book says more than anything else about what Chicago was, is and needs always to be.

I read all of these stories and gazed into these faces during one very entertaining sitting and I hope you will also. Enjoy.

The Human Factor

Can you imagine having instant replay in baseball? There have been a lot of changes in the game over the years and I've seen it all. I never in my wildest dreams thought that they would ever put lights here in Wrigley Field, but sure enough, now we have lights. I used to tell people that we'd never get an electronic main scoreboard, but I don't say that anymore. And now people are saying that baseball needs instant replays to help out the umps on close plays. Who needs instant replays? Everyone should be allowed to make a mistake now and then. I tell you, instant replay would ruin the sport. We've got to keep the "human factor" in baseball. Going to a game here at Wrigley Field should remind everyone of that.

I work in the only manually-changed scoreboard in professional baseball today and there's not one fan in this ballpark who's complaining. There are three of us inside the centerfield scoreboard and we update the stats as things happen here at the park, as well as post scores from around the league. We work really hard to keep up with the pace of the game. I'm proud to tell people what I do, and, to tell you the truth, we do a pretty good job around here. On rare occasion, we have been known to make an honest mistake, but shouldn't the sport of baseball accept a little bit of human error? I bet even Harry Caray would have a comment on this!

During a game a few years ago, the "human factor" came into play inside the scoreboard at Wrigley Field. It was a game against Cincinnati and we were getting beat bad. It was late in the game and everyone in the park, including us guys in the scoreboard, were hoping for a comeback—a big comeback. And then the moment came. As I recall, Ryne Sandberg came up to bat and, after a short face-off with the tough Reds southpaw, Tom Browning, hit a powerhouse home run, driving in three. Of course, this barely made a dent with the Cubs so far behind, but the fans were roaring with excitement.

As I always do when a score is made, I yelled up to the other guys and told them what changes to make to their section of the board. So I hollered, "Three runs!" Now, just as the inside of this metal box can get blazing hot, it can also get incredibly loud. When the fans start cheering and yelling, we can barely hear ourselves think. I'm looking down at the fans and they're ecstatic, and I'm thinking, boy, we've got some great fans here today! As the next

DEAN GRAZIER, WRIGLEY FIELD SCOREBOARD KEEPER

play of the game resumes, I get a phone call from Rick Fuhs, the *electronic* scoreboard keeper who works out of the press box on the other side of the field. "Hey, eh Dean…you've got eight runs scored this inning by the Cubs and that last one was a three. Talk to you later."

In all the excitement and noise, the guy upstairs had decided that eight runs had scored instead of the three I had hollered to him. Well, my partners and I got a little red-faced, and it wasn't from the heat. We quickly made the change and the Cubs went on to lose the game. To this day, I can't figure out how my partner upstairs had thought a team, even a team as great as our Cubbies, could score eight runs on one play.

But let me say it again, I wouldn't have it any other way. This scoreboard is something that just doesn't need fixing. I hope they can just leave it alone.

"Afterwards, I introduced myself to Dr. King and he said, 'So you're the person who kept calling the jail asking about me.'"

BARBARA PROCTOR

God, Help Us

Have you ever been out there on the grass in Soldier Field when the stands are empty? Do you know how vast that stadium seems? You really start to question whether there are enough people in the universe to fill it.

In 1964, I was part of a group of citizens from the Interfaith Council who decided to sponsor a small rally for Dr. Martin Luther King. Al Raby, an educator and civil rights activist here in Chicago, headed up the planning committee and ultimately decided upon Soldier Field as the ideal location for the event. At that point, of course, the small rally turned into an epic gathering. Though I didn't have any experience organizing something of that magnitude, I did have great enthusiasm, and was put in charge of public relations.

We tried from the start to get a nationally recognized assemblage of civil rights figures to host the event and we were quite successful. James Forman of the Student Nonviolent Coordinating Committee (SNCC), James Farmer of the Congress of Racial Equality (CORE), Fr. Theodore Hesbergh, the President of the University of Notre Dame, as well as the glorious Mahalia Jackson, all made early commitments to participate. As our initial concerns about who would appear behind the podium were settled, the realization that the endless space in front of the podium needed to be filled hit us hard. That was one of the scariest moments of my young life, seeing the infinitely huge and empty stadium in front of my wide eyes. But it was reality and it was better that I realized ahead of time just how many seats needed to be filled. Soon we were making phone calls all over the city and around the country, explaining the purpose and importance of this rally to all who would listen. The response was overwhelmingly positive. Hundreds of diverse groups from everywhere imaginable committed to sending hundreds and thousands of people, by car, by train, and mostly, by bus.

After much planning and anticipating throughout the spring, the week of the rally was finally upon us. Everything was moving along so smoothly that the rally seemed destined to be a great success. Then, to our distress, the Wednesday before the event, Dr. King was arrested in Montgomery and was refusing to leave jail. So there we were, three days away from a packed stadium and no guarantee that our "star" could or would attend! People

BARBARA PROCTOR, PRESIDENT OF PROCTOR & GARDNER ADVERTISING

from everywhere called to ask, "Are you going to postpone the rally? Is he going to be there?" We had no way of predicting the answer to the latter question, but with the tremendous logistical concerns involved with rescheduling an event like this, we crossed our fingers and said authoritatively as possible, that yes, indeed, the rally would proceed as planned. I must have called that jail every half-hour for updates on the situation. I was simply told time and again that Dr. King refused to come out. As a matter of principle, he would not leave.

As of Friday, Dr. King was still in jail and the situation appeared further and further from resolution. So, on Saturday morning, trembling, I went to Soldier Field with my life in my hands. I went up to the press box and what I saw was unbelievable. Like a caravan, an endless stream of buses rolled into the huge parking lot, and masses of people were starting to enter the gates and head toward their seats. Before my eyes, this incredible event was unfolding and yet there was no Dr. King. All these people, and no Dr. King.

The rally was supposed to get started around 10:30 a.m. but we waited in hopeful silence until about noon before we decided that something had to be done. Everybody was asking, "What are you going to do? What are you going to tell the press?" I just kept quietly praying, "Please God, get him here." Finally, we had no choice but to head down to the field and apologize to the crowd. Our heads were bent low as we started our descent when suddenly the south gates flew open and in came this white Cadillac convertible doing what seemed like 90 miles per hour. A beaming Dr. King was sitting up high in the backseat, waving to the crowd that was now on its feet. I had never been happier to see anyone in my whole life. Instantly, I was catapulted from the depths of despair and disappointment to an overwhelming excitement. I felt for a moment that I had actually willed him to be there, I had wanted it so dearly. From that amazing moment on, the day went along as originally planned, a few hours behind schedule, but we heard very few complaints.

Afterwards, I introduced myself to Dr. King and he said, "So you're the person who kept calling the jail asking about me." I explained the anxiety that I had been feeling as the rally was approaching and with a quiet smile he told me that he didn't want to let anybody down—just maybe worry them a little bit. He had succeeded. Press accounts of the rally estimated upwards of 75,000 people in attendance. *Jet* Magazine called it "the largest integrated civil rights rally" ever. I would add that in my mind it was also the most dramatic.

"I guess any city that claims as its title 'Second City' is not going to be considered second, but more like third or fourth."

JOE SEDELMAIER

JOE SEDELMAIER, FILM DIRECTOR AND PRODUCER

3

Is it Funny in Zurich?

When I first started in the business the conventional wisdom was that in order to make it you had to go someplace else—New York, Los Angeles, San Francisco, even Atlanta—definitely not Chicago. I guess any city that claims as its title "Second City" is not going to be considered second, but more like third or fourth. But I liked the quality of life here. It's easy to get around, there's the lake, a great symphony orchestra, second-hand bookstores, and colder-than-hell winters. Colder-than-hell winters saved this city. If Chicago had weather like Florida, we'd be L.A. and I wouldn't wish that on anybody.

I like to make funny commercials. Since 90 percent of my production is in Chicago, I'm often asked if Midwestern humor travels well. You see, there's a slot for everything and humor is no exception. There's Midwestern humor, Southern humor, West Coast humor, and East Coast humor (split into New England and New York humor). Then there's English humor, French humor, Japanese humor, German humor (formerly West German and East German humor), and so on.

I once did a commercial for an insulation product sold in France, Germany and Italy. The pitch was that by using this insulation you would save on your heating bills. Naturally, what you did with these savings was your business. So, we invented this man who saved enough money to buy 342 pink plastic flamingos. I cast Frank Markle, a retired actuary with the Presbyterian Church and lifelong Chicagoan, as the man. We posed Frank with the 342 flamingos on the front lawn of a house found in Rogers Park.

The completed spot was released with three different narrations: French, German, and Italian. When shown on the demo reels, we alternated the versions. Choice comments were: "those crazy French," "Germans have a weird sense of humor," and "that's an Italian front-yard if I ever saw one."

Which reminds me of the client who, thinking the name Sedelmaier was Jewish, called me a "pushy Jew." On being told it was German, he called me a "goddamn Nazi."

Cursed

I was made a Cub fan just like any other kid—I was cursed by my father. Why my father was a Cub fan, I don't know. We lived on the West Side, which, of course, was no man's land. If you lived on the North Side, you were a Cub fan. If you lived on the South Side, you were a Sox fan. The West Side was jump ball. I would actually get in fights with the kid down the block who was a Sox fan. It was weird. If you were from the West Side, you were kind of mixed up on this question.

It turned out I was mixed up about my age too. For the first 16 years of my life, I thought that my birthday was November 10th. Then, on my 16th birthday, I was going to go get my driver's license when my mother told me that I'd better first go and correct my birth certificate. My parents had changed my birth date so that they could send me to school at age four and my mother could go back to work. She was convinced that if she had told me any sooner, the government would have come in and sent me straight back to kindergarten. So I was never quite as old or as big as my classmates. Even though I loved baseball, I never really had much of a chance to get good at it. In high school, the boys around me seemed like men; I felt like a kid.

But I slowly learned that the jocks didn't have to be the only center of attention and soon I got my first taste of show business. It came through an English assignment which asked us to "demonstrate something about England." All the other kids were taking it so literally—three buddies and I thought that we'd be creative, and decided to bring to our English class the hottest British export of the decade, *The Beatles*. We put on some wigs and worked out a couple of lip-synced numbers. We actually weren't bad. Our teacher got a big kick out of it and decided that we were ready to perform in front of the whole school. So we started to get serious about it and got some suits made up without collars, fine-tuned our wigs, and called ourselves *The Weasels*. This time, we really performed the songs, and remember, this was at the height of Beatlemania. So when the curtain went up and they said, "Here they are ladies and gentlemen, *The Weasels!*," the audience went berserk. They were screaming and pulling their hair and climbing over seats. We just looked at each other and kind of shrugged our shoulders. When we finished the two Beatles songs we knew, the crowd demanded an encore, so we repeated the first song. By the end of the assembly, even with our limited repertoire, we had received offers to play at sockhops. So, we started to get even more serious and officially started a band, renaming ourselves *The Apocryphals*.

I didn't know how to play a damn thing. I was the singer. Eventually, the other band members taught me how to play bass and for the next few years, we played in some of the bigger clubs in Chicago. In '68, we were the warm-up band at the Kentucky State Fair in Louisville, along with a band called *The Missing Links*, whose three members were Walter Parazaider, Danny Seraphine, and Terry Kath. Shortly after meeting at the fair, we ran into Walter at the old Aragon Ballroom and he told us of his plans to start a band with horns and piano players. We told him, "Yeah, sure Walt, sounds great..." Of course, the band he formed went on to become *Chicago*, but at the time, we really thought he was nuts to add extra members to a group when most bands were trying to cut out guys! Soon after, I quit *The Apocryphals* and started to concentrate on acting.

Not too long ago, I ran into Walt Parazaider. Our two careers, which had headed off in different directions 25 years ago, had come full circle. It was at an auto show and I heard this heavy Chicago accent, "Hey, Joe Mantegna." I turn around, and there he was in a black leather jacket and hair down to his shoulders. It was great to see him again. Both of us live out in L.A. now, but there's no denying our Chicago blood. We get together and commiserate about the fact that you can't get a decent Italian beef within a thousand miles of our homes. I mean, what the hell is going on here?

"After months of hard work rehearsing in my parents' basement, the group was ready for our first job together. We went out and bought tailor-made sharkskin suits."

WALT PARAZAIDER

Sinatra and Me

I was only nine years old when my mom took me to see Frank Sinatra in "Young At Heart" at the *Chicago Theater* on State Street. She was a huge fan, so, I think we were making the trip more for her benefit than for mine. I just thought we were going to see a movie, so I was shocked when, after the film was over, Frank Sinatra himself stepped out from behind the curtain and began to sing "Young At Heart" with a band backing him up. Mom was probably aware that this was going to happen, but I had no idea that, after watching Sinatra in the movie, the man himself would appear before me. That he could stand there with a microphone and elicit such a reaction from the audience was not only exciting, but amazing.

I scanned the crowd to gauge the various levels of awe. I looked back toward Sinatra, nudged my mom, and naively said, "I could do that...I *want* to do that." Though in a trance of some sort, I vaguely recall my mom saying something about perseverance and hard work. But the audience's reaction was what I was interested in. It had given me such a rush, that I immediately wanted to be part of show business just like Frank. Being only nine, I couldn't understand or predict the commitment it would take to develop the musical talent necessary to make the journey from my house on the West Side to a stage like the *Chicago Theater*, but I was ready to start the trip.

My dad was a trumpet player, so I was exposed to the music world at a young age. Dad would sometimes jam with his band at our house. I remember going to see him play at Polonia Grove on the South Side when his band was hired to play for a company picnic. The highlight for me was to enjoy a strawberry soda and watch Dad's band play while people danced to everything from "Blue Moon" to a lively polka number. I also remember seeing him perform at the V.F.W. Hall in Berwyn, and again saw my dad provide entertainment that made so many people have a good time. The power of music over people never ceased to amaze me.

Dad finally managed to get some extra money so I could take music lessons. I took clarinet lessons and taught myself saxophone and flute. I played in orchestras, marching bands, rock 'n' roll bands, and dance bands. I eventually played in clubs in every part of

WALT PARAZAIDER, CO-FOUNDER OF THE MUSICAL GROUP, CHICAGO

town. My parents couldn't have picked a better place to raise me—Chicago was, and is, a melting pot for every type of musical style.

In the Spring of 1967, I received my degree in classical clarinet from DePaul and faced a difficult career choice: I could pursue a career as a clarinetist in the Chicago Symphony, or pursue something more musically dangerous. I had already formed a rock 'n' roll band with horns, made up of a mix of musicians from all over town. The city's musical influences and styles had brought together a group of people with high talent and diverse ideas. We named the band *The Big Thing* and started to have some fun. The classical career gradually became less of an option.

After months of hard work rehearsing in my parents' basement, the group was ready for our first job together. We went out and bought tailor-made sharkskin suits. It was a snowy March night when we pulled up with a U-Haul trailer full of equipment to *Club GiGi* in Lyons, Illinois. As we unloaded and set up our gear, our nervousness was masked by our excitement to actually play our first gig. We were extremely confident about what the band could do, and naively assumed that we were the best nightclub band ever to set foot in the place. Soon it was showtime. Our keyboardist was not only in charge of the keyboards, but the stagelights as well. When he hit the lights for the first show, we all realized that there was no one in the audience. I was the saxophonist and emcee for the band, so after the first song, I had the dubious honor of talking to the empty seats and welcoming all our guests to the show. The only audience was the owner and the hired help. After I got over the fear of talking to the empty seats, I began to enjoy this strange situation. We went ahead with the show as planned, playing our best material, telling our best audience-pleasing jokes, and doing our best choreography, copying the moves of James Brown and *The Temptations*. Halfway through the first set, we actually brought in a crowd of six, but they were all relatives.

When the set was over, we felt pretty good about our overall performance, despite the small crowd. We were backstage in the dressing room patting each other on the back when the club owner came in, took me aside and said, "You know I'm paying you guys top dollar and you have no show. Your music isn't good enough, and you'll never gain a following. You guys will never make it in the music business." I didn't agree with anything he said. The band forged ahead. In '69, shortly after our first record was released under the name *Chicago*

Transit Authority, we changed the band's name to simply *Chicago*. The sharkskin suits were history, but we were still playing with the same enthusiasm we had had back at *Club GiGi*. And the crowds were starting to swell beyond our wildest dreams.

The musical career I had envisioned to last for only a couple records and several years surprisingly has lasted for more than 25 years now. I never expected that a little idea for a rock 'n' roll band with horns would result in over 100 million of our records being sold. And I never dreamed that I would make the transition from playing for six people to a crowd of over 500,000.

Of all the honors we have received, one of the biggest came during the early '70s. We were enjoying the success of the band's song, "Colour My World," which topped the singles chart. Frank Sinatra approached us and wanted to record the song himself. He was a fan of ours and admired our music. I took it as an enormous compliment to the band that Frank Sinatra wanted to record our music. What Frank didn't know was that his performance years ago at the *Chicago Theater* had made me want to entertain people. Ironically, years later, *Chicago* was entertaining him. In my eyes, that wasn't too bad for a bunch of guys who "had no show" and would "never make it in the music business."

The Warmth of Her Touch

Have you ever felt a heart so warm that the touch of the person's hand could completely remove any chill from the wind on Michigan Avenue? That's my mother's heart and hand.

My favorite memories of Chicago are Christmas shopping with her on December 23rd or Christmas Eve. We would get off the subway at the Jackson Street stop and walk over to State Street. In and out of the shops—Carson Pirie Scott, Wieboldt's, Montgomery Ward and the little stores along the way. We would peer into the windows looking at the Christmas displays, the fairyland Christmas scenes. The shoemaker's hammer would go up and down on the play shoe, while the tiny mouse would stick his head out of the mouse hole. There was the fluffy fake snow strewn throughout the window and we began to count on each Christmas in Chicago to have at least some snow.

As we shopped little by little our bags became full. My mother gave me ten dollars to buy my presents for everyone. And I would look for exactly the right gift and ask her opinion. She gave me her sage advice, but made sure I made up my own mind. Mint candy for Ricky, gloves for my father; my sister Ada was always difficult.

Sometimes we would walk over to Michigan Avenue and look at the thousands of tiny bright lights that outlined the trees and up and down the streets. The wind would blow, and my mother held my hand and we both talked about how beautiful the Christmas lights were.

After twilight we would start heading home. Back to 65th and Drexel. I remember that it always seemed that the snow would start to fall and it got colder as we walked down the street. She would hold my hand and tell me to stomp my feet if they got cold.

But to this day, all I remember is the warmth from my mother's hand, my excitement about Christmas Eve, and the beautiful smile she always had for me.

My mother died yesterday and she was happy, intelligent, bright and enthusiastic. And I will always remember Michigan Avenue, State Street and Wabash on Christmas Eve and, despite the wind, how warm I was.

Dorothy Jemison, Mother, I love you.

RICHARD MELMAN, RESTAURATEUR

Love in November

There's a children's book about baseball I used to read to my kids that talked about the role of luck in getting a hit. "Lucky hats won't do it. Lucky bats won't do it. Only hard work will do it," said the story, and, in general, I believe that adage could be applied to pretty much anything you do in life, especially to the restaurant business. That said, I do believe there was a great deal of luck that came to me with the opening of my first restaurant, *R.J. Grunts*—luck that set in motion the success of *Lettuce Entertain You*, and my personal success beyond business.

R.J. Grunts opened in 1971, but not to blockbuster lines and rave reviews, no matter how history gets rewritten. At that point in my life, I wasn't cushioned financially or emotionally to accept its failure. The first few weeks of business were gloomy—40, 50, 60 customers for dinner, less than 20 at lunchtime. The original menu was primarily healthy, with fresh fruit shakes and no smoking permitted in the restaurant. But that was the '70s, not the '90s, and the customers were shocked. So burgers and fries quickly became highlighted on the menu, and smoking was allowed, but still the place was two-thirds empty. Nothing I tried seemed to have much effect, and my spirits were lower than the sales. For the first time, I started doubting myself.

The lucky part of opening *R.J. Grunts*, though, was this time of trial before it became an "overnight success." Part of the luck was picking the right partner to go into business with, who offered encouragement when I most needed it. That partner was the "J" in *R.J. Grunts*, Jerry Orzoff. Jerry gave me the unconditional love and confidence I couldn't give myself. When I was down, he was calm and supportive. He also gave me free reign to make whatever changes I wanted to, in order to turn *Grunts* around. I did everything I could think of, and most things people suggested, and it still seemed to me that the restaurant was going nowhere. I began to feel desperate, but Jerry, a most impatient man by nature, was patient and sure that success was still ours to have. And finally it was. One afternoon that summer, I took a trip to *Slicker Sam's* in Oak Park, where a semi-satisfied customer had suggested I could learn how to prepare dungeoness crab properly. As I returned to *Grunts*, I saw the first waiting line of customers ever. Jerry was there, smiling and victorious, and we were in business! I'll never forget how I felt when it seemed *Grunts* would fail, and I factor that memory and that fear of failure into every restaurant I open.

R.J. Grunts has brought me as much happiness personally as it has in business, and for that I feel extremely lucky. In addition to Jerry, who was my partner and my best friend until he died in 1981, in those early *Grunt's* years, I met many wonderful people who have added meaning and worth to my adult life. Of all the people who came through *Grunt's* revolving doors, though, the one who continues to share and shape my destiny is my wife, Martha. I met her in November 1972. By then, business was solidly good and had been for long enough that I was getting ready to think of things besides salad bars and work schedules.

The night I met Martha, I was standing at the host station with Jerry, discussing the fact that while the restaurant had been good to me in many ways, I hadn't met any women (unlike Jerry, who managed to meet four or five a day—but that's a different story). Jerry told me I needed to "open myself to the experience of meeting women," or something equally '70s in tone, and just then, Martha came through the aforementioned revolving door. Seventies or not, that was karma. It turns out, though, that I was too shy to act on my own karma, and Jerry had to take over. *He* made the introductions, *he* got Martha and her girlfriend a table, and *he* conducted the preliminary interview—"What's your name? Are you single? Where do you live? Do you need an apartment?" (He also worked in real estate.) When he tossed the conversational ball to me, I was still feeling so shy I spent most of the time looking at Martha, while talking to her girlfriend. It didn't seem to matter, though, because she and I somehow both realized we'd gotten lucky that night, not in the usual sense, but in a real, metaphorical one. We didn't fall in love in *R.J. Grunts* in November 1972, but we each changed the directions of our lives after that evening. When we met again, one year later, lightning struck and bells went off, and it was love at second sight, 'til death do us part.

People ask me all the time which of the restaurants is my favorite, and I always answer, "*R.J. Grunts.*" That's not because it's the most successful, though it's still going strong after more than 20 years; and it's certainly not the biggest or the most acclaimed. But, it brought me luck and love, and it opened the door to my entire adult life. It's been far better to me than any lucky hat or bat I could imagine.

"After many nice conversations with Juanita Jordan, I still hadn't been completely assured that Michael would be able to skip practice during the playoffs to join us at the beach. But I asked myself, how much does he really have to practice?"

SUGAR RAUTBORD

8

Waiting for Michael

It was a cold, blustery, wintery spring day and some of Chicago's most important corporate, civic, philanthropic, and artistic leaders were gathered together in gale force winds on the jetty just off North Avenue Beach to be photographed by Victor Skrebneski for *Town & Country*. Frank Zachary, the brilliant editor of the magazine, had finally decided to go ahead with an idea about which I had been tugging on his sleeve for years: to devote an entire issue to showing Chicago as the very *real* place it is, with an understanding that it's neither a cowtown nor simply a jazztown; it is a place with an exceptional range of culture. The epic photograph, which would extend across four pages, was intended to exemplify the dynamic spirit of the people of our city as depicted against the monumental, astounding cityscape.

My initial job was to somehow arrange for this to take place. Can you imagine the difficulty in trying to choose a date and time which was agreeable to the nearly four dozen people we wanted to include? The logistics were incredible. A typical conversation was as follows: "Can you come?" "What for?" "To stand on the lakefront for a group picture?" "Sugar, have you lost your mind? Have you gone mad?" I would then have to tell them that the Mayor and others had already agreed to be there. It often wasn't until I mentioned that Michael Jordan was going to be there, though, that many of them expressed real interest. Actually, after many nice conversations with Juanita Jordan, I still hadn't been completely assured that Michael would be able to skip practice during the playoffs to join us at the beach. But I asked myself, how much does he really have to practice?

Scheduling concerns were easy, however, compared to the negotiating I had to do on the editorial front. Some of the New York editors thought that it would be absolutely delightful —since it was Chicago, and all anyone ever knew about Chicago, being misinformed, was Mrs. O'Leary's cow and The Fire—to have an actual-size replica of the clumsy beast in the photograph! They somehow had overlooked the fact that one cannot get an accurate glimpse of this city's present commercial, intellectual, and artistic vibrancy by reviving an icon from 1871. Not to mention that this picture was to be taken by this extraordinary Chicago photographer, who certainly had never done livestock. Victor and I quietly decided to lose the cow. Each time I received a call from New York inquiring, "Did you get the cow yet?"

SUGAR RAUTBORD, AUTHOR AND SOCIALITE

I replied as innocently as possible that, "No, in fact, the cow has not yet arrived." With a call to my friend Sandy McNally of Rand-McNally, the bovine became instead a beautiful oversized globe upon which the Mayor could rest his elbow. We also were insistent that this photograph not be exclusively a social chronicle that would showcase our elite, but rather an inclusive image that showed the workers of this city who happen to wear blue collars alongside those who wear white. It was in this spirit that we asked individuals such as police officer Keith Mayo, construction worker Bruce Holaday, and a shop supervisor at Fannie May Candies, Rita Zacharias, to join us.

The day arrived maybe six weeks too quickly. All of the preparations were in place, yet Mother Nature hadn't heard of our plans. She made sure that the tea, crumpets, and flowers which a caterer had provided, were blown away before they could be much enjoyed. The dramatic skyline was shrouded in a dreary gray by clouds that tended to leak, and the great picture that we had planned seemed doomed. But, incredibly, at the appointed hour, out of the mist, they started to arrive. They arrived in limousines, they arrived on foot, and, in one case, they arrived by helicopter.

Mayor Daley and his wife, Maggie, Dick Duchossois, Ardis Krainik, Irv Kupcinet, Studs Terkel, Neil Bluhm, Minnie Minoso, Clarence Page, Edward Brennan, Bernard Brennan, Gertrude Crain, Bill Wirtz, Leon Lederman, Gene Siskel, and Roger Ebert, were just a few of the luminaries that found their way to our shoreline encampment. There were many introductions to be made and I was the extent of the welcoming committee, so I ran around doing my best to make everyone feel that they were in the right place and among friends. The sole concern that each and everyone seemed to share, after they had been there for a few minutes, was the question of where, after all, was Michael Jordan.

And then there was Victor, who usually made photographs in the rarified atmosphere of his studio against impeccable white seamless background, with soothing music, and where he reigns supreme in this very private universe where epiphanies happen. Suddenly, he was faced with a situation in which his equipment was literally being blown away and even with the benefit of three scarves and a policeman's jacket, he was catching pneumonia. "Sugar," he said as he handed me the bullhorn, "arrange them." So arrange them I did.

And, as I hurriedly gave directions to our guests, hoping to get going before the sprinkle turned into a shower, I had the simple realization that these were Chicagoans; there were no uncontrollable egos, no prima donnas. I had known many of them prior to this shoot, but there were many with whom I had become acquainted purely because of this picture, and I felt absolutely at ease with everyone present.

"Leon," I called through my new megaphone, "could you move a little to your left, into Maureen...incidentally, that is Mrs. Smith, who chairs the Art Institute's Women's Board." Nobel Prize-winning physicist meets chairwoman. In this same manner I continued to choreograph. But, again, everyone in the shot seemed to be concerned not with the threat of a downpour and not with their particular position in the photograph, but with the question of how long to wait for Michael Jordan. The general consensus was that we should wait as long as necessary, even if it meant getting a bit damp.

But, of course, we had to move along. At the last moment, I turned over the megaphone to Victor, and the walkie-talkie (with which we had been helping to position the helicopter in the background) to an assistant, and I joined those to be photographed, representing the Chicago-based Alzheimer's Association. Everyone looked into the famous lens, smiled, and in a few flashes, it was over.

A wonderful group of Chicagoans had come together graciously and willingly, if only for a moment, to show the world that they love this city, they believe in this city, and they'll work hard for this city, even if that means standing along the lakefront for a group picture under less than ideal conditions. All that was left to do was to say goodbye and head back towards one's own mode of transportation, whether it involved wheels, feet, or rotor blades. But most of the group lingered momentarily. How much longer, after all, could basketball practice last?

Hungry for the Blues

September, 1957. The first train I'd ever been on brought me to Chicago. I didn't know a soul. My mother was paralyzed, living in Louisiana, and I came here looking to do two things; one was to make some music, and the other was to make some money. I wandered the streets looking for common day labor, but I wasn't finding much work and I wasn't having much luck with the music business either. Days would go by and I wouldn't have anything to eat.

Six o'clock in the evening months later, I was at a pay phone, ready to call home and tell 'em I was on my way back. In those days you still needed a dime to make a collect call and that was all I had, a dime and my guitar. But I'd never pawn my *Les Paul*, never. As I was standing there this man walked up, started talking to me, and asked me if I could play the blues. I told him, "I'll play you some blues if you buy me a hamburger." The man just laughed and said, "Look, I'm a country man and I know if you feed the dog he won't hunt for you. But, if you can play the blues, I'll give you some wine." I had never had much to drink and I said "Look, what I need is a hamburger," but wine was all he offered. I don't remember much except going to this guy's house and doing a lot of playing and singing. I remember him saying to his wife, "Get ready because this little s.o.b. can *play*."

From there, he took me to the famous *708 Club* at 708 East 47th Street. I must have looked like a child walking in there. He pointed to the guy who was playing up on the stage and said to him, "This man here can run you off the stage." Well, the man up on the stage, who I didn't know at the time, was Otis Rush. Otis just looked down at us both and said, "Bring him up." So I got up there and played "Things That I Used To Do" and "Further On Up The Road." The owner of the club, who usually only came around to pick up the night's receipts, happened to be there and on his way out said to the manager, "Whoever that is up there, hire him."

During all of this, people kept asking me "Who are you? Where are you from?" All I was trying to do is get back to a pay phone so I could call home. The wine the man had given me was long gone and I was telling everybody how hungry I was, but nobody was doing anything about it.

After 20 minutes of nobody paying me any attention, this big man with high cheek bones came up to me, grabbed me by the collar and started shaking the hell out of me. Everyone in the club seemed to know who he was—sounded like they were calling him *The Mud*. But after a few shakes the bells started ringing in my head and I thought they were saying "He's getting *mugged*." I remember thinking this is it—this is when my guitar gets stolen. So I'm blubbering and pleading and he just looked down at me and said, "Settle down, I'm Muddy Waters." And I said, "You're who?" and he said "I'm Muddy Waters. These fine people called me at home and got me out of bed to come see you. Someone said you're hungry." I said, "If you're really Muddy Waters, I'm not so hungry." He laughed, and handed me a salami sandwich, saying, "Now quit worrying about your stomach, and don't think about going home."

Since I had arrived in Chicago, I'd watched the sky and saw all the birds flying south. I thought of the phrase "birdbrain" because I was beginning to think these birds had more sense than I did. But after I met Muddy Waters, then Howlin' Wolf, Little Walter, Junior Wells, Jimmy Rogers, Magic Sam, Willie Dixon, and Sonny Boy Williamson, there was no longer the need to head south because, the way these guys played, it never seemed to get cold. My body might have felt it, but the voice inside of me told me that I couldn't leave the life I loved. I knew I owed it to myself to stay where the greatest musicians in the world were, where every night I could go listen to—or play—the music that I loved.

"I met him in Champaign.
An odd place for a Hungarian
to be. He acknowledged he
had made a terrible mistake.
He'd never heard of Illinois
in Hungary, and assumed it
had rolling hills and a good
climate."

NICOLE HOLLANDER

I am Brave, I am a Chicagoan

I find myself driving on March 21st...driving on the Edens Expressway in a blinding snowstorm 25 miles an hour, at two in the afternoon with my lights on; I'm trying to keep my nerve. It's the first day of spring and I have picked this day to visit my mother in a northern suburb. It's clear that everyone on the highway is as terrified as I am because, although each of us are continually changing lanes, we're doing it at a snail's pace, hoping to find the lane where it's not snowing. No one is honking their horns. People are exhibiting a kind of hysterical politeness that is seldom seen in Chicago, unless there is an emergency.

Some people have pulled off the highway and are trying to clean off their windshield wipers, some have abandoned their cars on the off-ramps. Where do those people go? Do they knock on the doors of houses near the expressway? Do people let them in? I am wondering how I got to be 52 and am still foolish enough to be driving in a snowstorm.

I turn on the radio for courage and hear Neil Tesser on WBEZ saying, "You know it's spring when the election signs are covered by their first layer of snow." A familiar refrain runs through my head: Why am I still here?

When I was growing up I knew of only two people who had moved away from Chicago. One was my cousin Gail who was ripped from the arms of my Aunt Belle by her father, who arrived by train in the middle of the night and took her off to live in Southern California. The other person also left town in the middle of the night. Harry was our downstairs neighbor. He made his living loaning money to gamblers and was foolish enough to skim money from his gangster boss, whose name was "Something, the Camel Humphrey." Harry and family fled to a primitive city that didn't have delis or Chinese restaurants on every corner...Baltimore.

Everyone else I knew lived in Chicago, and continued to live in Chicago until they died. If they wanted a change of scenery, say in the summer, they went to Union Pier, Michigan, or Lakeside, Michigan if they were wealthy. When did it first occur to me that I could leave this city and find one where the sun shone even in February? I didn't think of it when the time came to attend college. I had no idea that I could go any farther from home than Champaign, Illinois. I didn't know that getting far, far away from home where you can act out in a pleasant climate, is one of the best reasons for an advanced education.

NICOLE HOLLANDER, CARTOONIST, CREATOR OF SYLVIA

It must have occurred to me around age 21, because I'm pretty sure the reason I got married was because I believed a man would quite literally take me away from all of this. It was 1956 and I married a man with a foreign accent. Maybe I thought he would take me really far away.

I met him in Champaign. An odd place for a Hungarian to be. He acknowledged he had made a terrible mistake. He'd never heard of Illinois in Hungary, and assumed it had rolling hills and a good climate. He wanted to leave as soon as he arrived. In the '50s, marriage was the necessary first step to leaving the state. My mother couldn't object to my going off with my new husband, even though her heart was broken and she didn't get what I saw in him anyway. I left Chicago and went east.

I'd never even learned to drive, I didn't need to. Chicago had a great public transportation system, street cars, buses, even double-decker buses, the El and the subway. I didn't even ride a bike. I was a pedestrian.

In my married state, I was able to travel to Princeton, New Jersey—"The Garden State"—but cold, and then abroad to England—rainy—but lush; Paris and Florence, all in the winter, finally ending up in Germany—very, very cold. Their coldest winter in many years they said. I feared cold was my karma.

Finally, we left Europe and moved to Cambridge, Massachusetts. Chicago was behind me, but not winter. Surely something was wrong. Perhaps it was my husband? We divorced and I prepared to move to the warm place of my dreams.

I didn't long to see the pyramids along the Nile or visit exotic islands or experience New York. I went west…to California, in search of sun and trees that looked like our house plants, but big as houses. I imagined horseback riding on white beaches (not me of course, but I would view it from under a beach umbrella) and a new, sunnier, happier self.

My first sight of Berkeley was disappointing. Surely these feeble shacks weren't architecture, only some kind of temporary shelter, little better than tents, on a par with the summer cottages of my childhood. Buildings were brick. Made to last, built to shelter immigrants and their practical children. Real buildings had hallways, an oasis between the frigid cold of the outside and the overheated inside. And California politics seemed so pallid compared to Chicago's—jobs that paid good money in Chicago were filled by volunteers in California—volunteers!

In California, I had a series of heartbreaks. I lost a love and couldn't find work. Soon, the beauty of my surroundings was obscured by my sobbing. I did learn to drive, but I couldn't see the road through my tears. So out of love and unemployed, I came back to the city where if you can't make it there you can't make it anywhere.

I had missed the Democratic Convention of 1968 and the riots, but I came back in time to join the National Organization of Women and be among those marching in the St. Patrick's Day parade, as a Chicago Irish Feminist. That day I had my first experience of walking in a parade, in a freezing drizzle, behind horses.

What if I had stayed out in California, a place where people slept out in the open campgrounds whenever they had a chance, and I never got to experience opening day at Wrigley Field, when men remove their shirts and expose their large pale bellies to the sun. There's no other city where people rush so foolishly into t-shirts and shorts at the first sign of spring. I was happy to be home again. I had missed that edgy Chicago sense of humor, those thick friendships honed to perfection during long winters. You can't duck out on your relationships in Chicago and take a long walk; it's too cold to give up your friends.

After a while I got restless again. I'd become a cartoonist and I thought of a new way to look for a warm place to live. I would give lectures at universities that were located in towns where it was warm in the winter. Though terrified to speak in public and paralyzed with fear by the thought of airline food, I would travel to new cities and towns and stay in fine hotels.

I visited Los Angeles, and Boulder, and the Carolinas, and Sarasota, Florida…even Bozeman, Montana. My longing for warmth drew me to Southerners who had come to Chicago, and when they were seduced back home to the South, I visited them in Eureka Springs, Arkansas, Tampa, Key West, and Savannah, Georgia.

It's bitter cold and snowing today. I peek through my window. I'm planning to stay home in bed with a good mystery, when I spy battalions of old ladies, tough as brazil nuts, trudging through snow, dragging their shopping carts behind them. Can I do less? My mother calls me and says: "You're not going out today are you?" and I say, "just to the corner for a quart of milk." She sighs. In weather like this, she says, the moisture in your eyeballs can freeze. I go anyway, I am brave, I am a Chicagoan. Surely, I can be brave somewhere else, in some other way. I might leave town for good at any moment.

CHRISTIE HEFNER, CHAIRMAN AND CEO, PLAYBOY ENTERPRISES, INC.

11

The Whole Truth

After my mother and father separated in 1955, my mother, brother and I moved to an apartment building in the 5800 block of North Sheridan Road, about as close to the lake as you could live without getting wet. I was blonde as a kid from all the hours I spent out in the sun at the beach.

I attended grammar school farther north, at National College of Education, now known as National-Louis University. It was a small, progressive, superb school. Because it was affiliated with the teachers college, the program it offered was individualized and ahead of its time. For example, I remember playing the title role when my fifth grade class performed "Sleeping Beauty" completely in French! The class sizes were comfortable, with fewer than 20 kids in each grade, so my classmates and I got to be pretty good friends.

One afternoon I was playing with one of my girlfriends and she innocently asked me about my Dad. I told her in a very matter-of-fact way that he was the editor of *Playboy* magazine. This was in 1961, so both the magazine and I were nine years old. I never thought anything more of it, nor did she ever mention it again.

After more than 20 years of not seeing or hearing from each other, my friend called me, and we had a reunion lunch. Over food and wine at *Gordon's* restaurant, she told me that after our exchange that day so many years ago, she had gone home and repeated exactly what I'd said about my Dad to her parents, only to get herself in trouble. Her mother's response was, "Now don't go believing everything your little friends tell you!"

Of course, we both laughed about the incident, but I've wondered since my lunch, at what point they figured out that I *had* been telling the truth, and often imagined what her parents might have thought.

Now, I wonder how many other little friends I inadvertently got into trouble…

Stoppard, Chekov, Mamet, and Me

There aren't too many people who get a chance to reassess their life after they've lived half of it, essentially saying that the first half was a mistake, and another course should be tried. But that's what I did. And I don't know that I could have done it anywhere else.

As a child growing up in England, I'd been a member of the *Stratford Children's Theater*. At 12, I was already a character actor, always Polonius—never Hamlet. When I immigrated to the United States at 20, sponsored by my sister, I figured the age of responsibility had arrived. Acting would have to be set aside for something less risky. During the six years I went to school to earn my degrees in English, I supported myself by working in a hospital as an orderly. Upon graduation I became a teacher, a profession, it turned out, I wasn't particularly good at and didn't especially enjoy. So I did what any master degreed former teacher with hospital experience would do: I went to work editing medical journals.

Every workday for too many years, I walked into the Hancock Building to perform what had become my life's work, writing about cataracts and cardiology, hemorrhoids and hematomas. My heart just wasn't in it. By the time I hit 35, I knew that something was wrong, something—I couldn't put my finger on what—was missing in my life. It was truly a troublesome, scary time for me. I'd come home and plop down in front of the television and start to make my way through a six-pack of beer and four packs of cigarettes. Something had to change.

Two years later, in 1977, I took a trip to England to see my family. While there, I went to the *National Theater* in London to see Tom Stoppard's play "Jumpers," and something just exploded in my mind. My God, this is it, I thought, this is what is missing! This is what I have to do again. I had been on stage so many years ago though, was I now too old? I went to Manchester and was able to see Leo McKern in "Uncle Vanya." I was so taken by his performance that I went back the next day to buy tickets so that I could see him again. I walked into this little coffee shop next to the box office and there sat Leo McKern himself, unshaven and a bit disheveled, eating a sausage roll and drinking tea. It was exactly what I needed to see; the "gods of the stage" were, off-stage, human just like me, with feet most often firmly planted on the ground. When I got back home to Chicago, I immediately went to see "A View from the Bridge" at the *St. Nicholas Theater*, an experience that confirmed what I really already knew. I had rediscovered my calling and was ready to climb back into the world and try again.

If, at age 37, I had decided to become an actor and had been living in Los Angeles, it wouldn't have worked. Same with New York. In either city, if a director wants a 22-year-old blonde with one blue eye and one brown eye who happens to be a Gemini with a Virgo ascending, they'll get 500 at the audition who fit the bill. In 1977 in Chicago, without the crowds, a renaissance was taking place. There existed a flexibility and fluidity that was unlike other places. Actors and actresses got a chance to stretch. If a part was written as male and the best person for the part was female, a change was made: Henry, more often than once, became Henrietta. I enrolled in acting classes at *St. Nicholas'*, surrounded by twenty-somethings, and was slow to get a feel for it again, and felt awkward. But soon I had confirmation that I was improving. David Mamet cast me in his new play, "The Water Engine."

Over the course of a decade, it became a matter of tremendous prestige to claim Chicago as being the city of your theatrical roots. Many times in other cities, I've seen actors who are about as Chicago as Al Pacino, look into the eyes of their auditioners and, with their best Chicago accent, claim affiliation with *Steppenwolf* or *The Goodman*. Chicago's reputation as a place that produces actors and actresses of the highest caliber is ironic when you consider the opinions of the hometown fans. More than once, people have come up to me on the street here at home and say, "I loved you in such and such…what are you doing in town?" When I say, well, I live here, they say, "oh," and I see their faces fall as they silently say, "*I thought you were a real movie star.*" But Chicago's been home to me since I got here, and I think it always will be. It's where I get my strength. If by living here I somehow never make the status of real movie star, somehow that's okay. The idea of being human, and having my feet firmly on the ground, has always been more important.

"The Country Club was,
our parents told us, restricted,
which meant closed to Jews.
It was more a mysterious
than a disturbing landmark.
It held down the south-eastern
corner of my world."

DAVID MAMET

DAVID MAMET, WRITER, PLAYWRIGHT AND DIRECTOR

Seventy-first and Jeffrey

The neighborhood from 71st Street north to the park was, in my youth, a Jewish neighborhood.

My grandmother took me shopping and spoke in what could have been Yiddish, Polish, or Russian to several shopkeepers on 71st Street. She even knew one or two of them from the Old Country, which was the town of Hrubieszów, on the Russian-Polish border. We lived on Euclid Avenue in a brick house.

There was a policeman, or guard, hired by some sort of block or neighborhood association, and his name was Tex. He patrolled the street, with two stag-handled revolvers on his belt; one worn butt forward, and the other worn butt-to-the-rear. He would stop and chat at length with us kids.

We spent as much time as possible out in the street. The manhole covers did duty for second base and home plate, or the two end zones, as the season demanded.

We would stay out far past dark in the summertime chasing each other around the neighborhood in what we called a "bike chase," which, if memory serves, was some version of the war game the New Yorkers called "ringalevio."

We loved being outside. We went looking for lost golf balls at the city's Jackson Park course, four blocks to the north; and we would trek in the park all the way over to the lake, where we'd look over at the South Shore Country Club.

The country club was, our parents told us, restricted, which meant closed to Jews. It was more a mysterious than a disturbing landmark. It held down the south-eastern corner of my world.

Coming back west down 71st was the Shoreland Delicatessen, and the next oasis following was J. Leslie Rosenblum, "Every Inch a Drugstore."

Rosenblum's was, to me, a place from a very different world. I found the style of the name foreign and distinctly un-Jewish in spite of the surname. The store itself was, if I may, the Apollonian counterbalance to the Ashkenazic Dionysia of the Shoreland.

Rosenblum's was cool, and somewhat dark and quiet.

Its claim to my attention was a soda fountain, which smelled of chocolate and various syrups and that indefinable rich coolness coming off the marble which, I fear, must remain unknown to subsequent generations. My Dad took me there for Chicago's famous chocolate phosphate.

I would like to conclude the gastronomic tour of South Shore with mention of the Francheezie. That *ne plus ultra* of comestibles was the product of the Peter Pan Restaurant, then situated in the corner of 71st and Jeffrey Boulevard, the crossroads of South Shore. The Francheezie was a hot dog split down the middle, filled with cheese, and wrapped in bacon; and, to be round, it was good.

The other spots of note to my young mind were the two movie theaters; the Hamilton to the east and the Jeffrey to the west of Jeffrey Boulevard. The latter was a block and a half from my house.

On Saturdays I'd take my quarter and get over to the movie house. The cartoons started, I believe, at 9 a.m., and there were so many of them. The phrase I remember is "100 Cartoons."

At seven minutes per, I calculate that they would occupy almost 12 hours, and that can't be right; but I prefer my memory to my reason. In any case, there were sufficient cartoons to keep the kids in the movie theater until past dark on Saturday, and that is where we stayed.

The Jeffrey and the Hamilton both boasted large, blue dimly lit domes set into their ceilings, and my young mind would many times try to reason what their use might be. I found them slightly Arabic, and 40 years later, can almost recall the fantasies I had gazing at them. I believe one of the domes had stars, and the other did not.

We had lemonade stands in the summer, and we trick-or-treated in the fall to the smell of the leaves burning in everyone's yard.

I remember fistfights at Parkside School, and the smell of blood in my nose as I got beaten by the friend of a friend, for some remark I'd made for which I think I'd deserved to get beaten.

Years later, long after we'd moved away, I lived up on the North Side.

I drove a Yellow Cab out of Unit 13, on Belmont and Halsted, and I got a fare to a deserted area, where I got a knife put to my throat and my receipts stolen.

The fellow took the money and ran off. I lit a cigarette and sat in the cab for a while, then drove off to look for a cop. I told the cop what had happened, and suggested that if he wanted to pursue the robber, I would come and help him, as the man couldn't be too far away.

He nodded and started writing down the information he required. I told him my name and he asked if I was related to the people who used to live in South Shore; and it turned out he'd bought our house. We talked about the house for awhile, and what it had been like, and how it had changed; and we both agreed the robber would be long gone.

I drove off in the cab, and that was my last connection with the old neighborhood.

14

Too Many Cooks?

The old saying about too many cooks spoiling the broth never made much sense to me. I used to do most of the cooking myself, but these days, I try to make sure I don't get too lonely in the kitchen. A lot has changed around here since we first took over the place more than 25 years ago, not only within our own walls, but around the neighborhood as well.

My husband and I came to Chicago from Poland in 1952, with three children. We didn't know anyone. Our train arrived at what I now know is Union Station, where I left my husband and children and went out in search of an apartment. Finding an apartment turned out to be the easy part; the hard part was trying to remember and explain where I had left my family. I knew very little English, but with the help of a cabdriver, I raced from station to station until I found the right one. I had found an apartment and found my family. Unfortunately, the little amount of luggage we had brought didn't find us. We left the train station without anything except literally the clothes on our backs, and headed for our new home near 18th and Damen.

We scraped along with very little. Sometimes my husband and I found ourselves on the edge of desperation trying to feed our children. One day it was so bad, I had to go to the corner grocer and ask for food I couldn't pay for right away. Winnie Waszlowski owned the store, and she seemed to understand my situation. She provided us with food and a basket of clothes donated by nuns. Years later, I tried to repay Winnie for her kindness and compassion while my family had been struggling by setting her up with one of the three bachelor butchers who had a shop down the street. Winnie just laughed. We became good friends.

As the children got older and were more able to take care of themselves, I got a job at a packing house near the stockyards. I knew immediately that I wasn't cut out for that kind of work, and started to dream of earning a living by doing something I loved—cooking. The dream paid off in 1965. After years of saving, my husband and I purchased the little place known as the *Busy Bee* from Berna Anderson, who held the mortgage for us. In the first few years I did everything from mopping the floors to doing the dishes. But I'm not ashamed to have once done those chores; I'm proud. I really believe that if you are

SOPHIE MADEJ, OWNER OF THE BUSY BEE RESTAURANT

determined to succeed in America and willing to work hard, you will make it.

Sophie's Busy Bee has always attracted a diverse group of diners—all different types. Abbie Hoffman used to eat here regularly during his days in Chicago, often not too far from a pair of policemen. And there was the bag lady who slept in Wicker Park across the street that would walk over every morning when we opened at six to get a cup of coffee and warm up. Some of the guys here pitched in to buy her a thick winter coat. She got offended for some reason and wouldn't take it. After years of coming in, the poor woman was hit by a car and killed right in front of the restaurant. They went through her scattered belongings and found more than $60,000! Very different kinds of people come through our doors.

But meeting different kinds of people from different places and with different ideas is what makes life so interesting and America so appealing. I don't tell many people that after a long day of preparing Polish sausage and pierogis, nothing sounds quite as good to me as take-out Chinese.

"I grew up thinking that *Mare-Daley* was the term for '*leader of the city.*' I thought that John Lindsey was New York's *Mare-Daley* and Tom Bradley was L.A.'s *Mare-Daley.*"

AARON FREEMAN

15

News Today, Comedy Tonight

I grew up believing that *Mare-Daley* was the term for "leader of the city." I thought that John Lindsey was New York's *Mare-Daley* and Tom Bradley was L.A.'s *Mare-Daley*. It never occurred to me while growing up that my political opinions mattered. All that mattered were the opinions of the Cook County Democratic Central Committee. My mother became a Republican for a time after she heard that Chicago's *Mare-Daley* received 270 votes in our precinct of 216 registered voters. It really seemed that the Democratic Party, "The Machine," controlled just about everything.

My interest in politics really started with Jane Byrne. Like many others, I'm sure, it never occurred to me that she might become mayor. I was just so pissed off, I voted for her. Same thing with Harold Washington—initially I just voted for him. When he won the primary it was a major shock. It dawned on me at that point that he could actually be elected. I immediately joined the campaign, working the 16th Precinct, 44th Ward, right along the lake. I passed out leaflets that said, "Even though he's a convicted criminal you should still vote for him." And then much to my amazement and surprise, he won! I went to my rooftop and screamed.

After Harold was inaugurated, everyone started to talk about the big council meeting—the big showdown. Well it turned out to be a very disappointing meeting for all the fans of Harold because Eddie Vrydolyak had arithmetic on his side. The following day, Vrydolyak's "Twenty-nine" had a public meeting and the majority of those in attendance were city and county workers. After attending both meetings, I was struck by the differences between the two leaders, each of them possessing a very different kind of clout. Harold seemed to have really enthusiastic supporters who really believed in him, while Vrydolyak had entrenched, Machine-type operators in his corner. My thought was that there was a bright side of "the clout" and a dark side of "the clout."

"Council Wars," as it came to be known, was a parody of *Star Wars* using city council members as the inspiration: Harold Skytalker, Darth Vrydolyak, C3 Pucinski, Obie Wan Oberman, Jesse Jack-Solo, Jabba the Burke, were just a few of the main players in the piece. It chronicled the epic struggle to get Harold seduced by the dark side of the clout and became

AARON FREEMAN, COMEDIAN, RADIO AND TELEVISION TALK SHOW HOST

so well-known that "Council Wars" became the generic term the media used for the city council standoff. Most of the real-life characters reacted to their new personas with a sense of humor. The only politicians to really complain were the ones who weren't important enough to be mentioned, though I did hear that Vrydolyak started to dislike me after Harold Washington, both privately and publicly, started calling him "Darth." And die-hard Harold fans thought it was inappropriate to make fun of the Mayor, especially to poke fun at his penchant for using big words. My response was, but he *does* use big words. In *Council Wars* we had a bit about Harold, in his capacity as a lawyer, forgetting to show up in court to represent a client. As Harold Skytalker, he responds, "I must discover some method to ameliorate my recollective capabilities..."

Looking back on that time, it seems inevitable that the two warring parties were to be relegated to opposite sides of "the clout." Local politics these days are relatively amorphous, making it harder to live up to my motto: If it's news today, it's comedy tonight!

"From my first left-winger, Ted Lindsey, came the wisest words of professional advice: 'Hit 'em first.'"

STAN MIKITA

STAN MIKITA, HALL OF FAME CHICAGO BLACKHAWKS HOCKEY PLAYER

16

Black and Blue

Not many people seem to remember that a few decades ago, Chicago Stadium was really a decrepit, dirty place. When I arrived here in 1958, a resident watchdog, a mean son-of-a-bitch named Bruno, ran the place. Everyone called him "Sir" on their way in at Gate 3-1/2. The locker rooms had warped wooden floors, and instead of lockers, they had nails all over the walls for the players to hang their clothes on. We would kid each other that if you didn't get hurt out on the ice there was no doubt you'd have an injury waiting for you in the dressing room. But the chances were pretty good that the ice would get you; the surface here at the Stadium was about on the same level as the warped wood. Some days you'd have slush, other days you'd have chunks flying up at you while you were skating. I don't know whether the problem was caused by impurities in the water or if the cooling system was just lousy. I just know that the condition of the ice slowed down a team that was small but potentially fast.

I came to the Blackhawks from an amateur league team in St. Catharines, Ontario, as a replacement for an All-Star player who had just been injured. Eighteen years old, and hadn't spent much time in big cities—Toronto was about the extent of my urban experience—I took an overnight bag and my own skates on an all-night train into the La Salle Street Station, not knowing who was going to be there to meet me. Nobody, as it turns out, at least not right away. There I was, a kid in a strange city, not knowing where the hell I was, not knowing who I was supposed to meet, and not knowing what to do. So I stopped in at the coffee counter and had a cigarette. About halfway through it I saw the coach, Rudy Pilous, making his way toward me. "You want to be a big leaguer or what?" he roared. "Put out that goddamn cigarette." He drove me over to the Stadium and set me up with some equipment, and then told me that I'd be staying for the time being with Bobby Hull. That was good news. Bobby and I had played hockey together for a few years in Canada and were friends. I asked Coach Pilous how to get to Bobby's house. "Well, you see that street out there? It's called Madison Street. You see that corner? That's a bus stop." "But which way do I go?" I asked him. "Go that way." he said pointing. "Go west. Go as far west as that bus will take you. Bobby will meet you there." "What if I end up in California?" "Don't worry, kid, you won't," he said as he waved me off. Of course, when I got off the bus after it made the U-turn at Austin Avenue, Bobby wasn't there, he was never known to be on time. He showed up a few cigarettes later and took me to his place out in Berwyn. We ended up rooming together for the next two years.

From my first left-winger, Ted Lindsey, came the wisest words of professional advice: "Hit 'em first." For the first couple years in the league those were words I played by. Hell, I was 152 pounds and 5' 8", so the type of hitting I did was more like jumping up and hitting 'em in the kneecaps. But either they were going to kill me and carry me out in a box, or I was going to survive. Luckily, I survived. For a string of years early in my career, I had the honor of being the most penalized player in the league. But this town always likes a spunky player.

After the summer of 1960, the team came back to a transformed Stadium. The whole place had been renovated and was almost unrecognizable—even the outside of the building had been cleaned up. None of us could get over the dressing room with real linoleum floors, even some carpeting, and fresh paint and paneling on the walls. Maybe Michael and Bill Wirtz finally decided the Blackhawks were ready to become a power in the National Hockey League. They must have. Besides the work on the building, they became the first guys to use distilled water on the ice surface, improving the conditions out there tremendously. Consequently, we became a faster, better skating team. Turned out that the condition of the building was tied in with the condition of the ice. When those were improved, the team improved and the fans started coming back. We probably filled about half the seats when I first got here. The '61 season started the road back to the loud, sold-out houses you see today. That year, we didn't disappoint anyone who came out to watch us—not the fans and not the Wirtzes. We won the Stanley Cup that year for the first time since 1938.

I headed back to Canada after that Championship season because that's what everyone did in those days. But once I got there, I realized that, other than my parents, I didn't have much to go back to. I decided that Chicago might be a good place to settle down and before long, I married a girl from the far West Side. Our kids were born here and I became, though not quite a native, hopefully an adopted native.

"I didn't relish living in a town where middle-aged women wear rhinestone-studded jumpsuits and look like extras on *Dynasty*"

TIM KAZURINSKY

17

Searching for Babushkas

I'd been working in New York for a few years, doing *Saturday Night Live*, not having nearly as much fun as you'd think. I only rented sublets in Manhattan—always kept my place here. I could never commit to New York. I guess it's the most exciting place on earth, but who needs that much excitement? I'd fly home every time we got a week off. As the plane would ease down at O'Hare, so would my shoulder muscles. For reasons I'd be hard-pressed to explain—even to myself—I had an abiding affection for this big, dopey city.

My friend, Bernie Sahlins, reckons Chicago's the greatest "make it" town in the world. He might be right. I got lucky here in the ad biz. Then I took a class at *Second City* and quickly wound up on the stage. John Belushi saw me there, waved his hand, and got me hired at *Saturday Night Live*. So now I was an actor on the hip TV show, and the pressure was on. Careerwise, I was advised I had two options; move to New York, or move to Los Angeles. I was already unhappy in New York. Los Angeles? I didn't relish living in a town where middle-aged women wear rhinestone-studded jumpsuits and look like extras on *Dynasty*. (Try to find a babushka in L.A.)

So it's Christmas. I figure I'll go shopping at Marshall Field's—gawk at the windows, see the tree. As I'm walking down Randolph Street, it's snowing like a bitch. Dirty slush everywhere. In front of Field's, a line of cabs covered in muck…waiting for package-laden shoppers to splurge. Three cabbies are on the sidewalk, cleaning crud off their front windshields with rags and scrapers. The first cabby, straining as he leans over his Yellow Checker, sings, "Tote dat barge…" The second cabby joins in, singing, "Lift dat bale…" The third cabby jumps in and, in unison, they boom, "Get a little drunk…and ya land in jail." They couldn't sing the chorus. They were laughing too hard. As were the passers-by. It was just a little thing. It was over in a moment. But I remember thinking to myself, "I gotta find a way to stick around this town. Hell…maybe I could write."

DENISE DECLUE, SCREENWRITER

Cherries Jubilee

Zahour's parents were Czechoslovakian, but he was a Chicagoan and proud of it. We met in journalism school at the University of Missouri and he invited me home to meet his sister. I said, "Great. I know a writer up there, maybe I can look him up." "What writer?" he scoffed, "Saul Bellow?" "No," I said, "Nelson Algren." Zahour went berserk. Algren was the best writer of the 20th century, the only guy who ever captured the true soul of Chicago, champion of the dispossessed, hero of the downtrodden, enemy of the powers-that-be, and to Zahour, basically, God.

I'd read *A Walk on the Wild Side* and *The Man With the Golden Arm* after I met Algren at a writers' conference in Boulder in '69. At first I thought he was just a big blow-hard. One night at a fancy dinner with other fancy writers, he, well, started to make fun of me. Maybe I should order some "*Cherries* Jubilee" for dessert. Did I like *cherries?* Did my date (a dealer from Vegas, who had written a story Algren adored—about picking crab lice out of his crotch) like *cherries?* Wink, wink. Nudge, nudge. Presumably, this had something to do with my youth and palpably virginal demeanor. Everybody but me thought it was hilarious.

Algren moved on to another subject, holding forth to worshipful attention while I stared at my Cherries Jubilee and the whipped cream that came with it. I was kinda nervous 'cause I'd only met the card dealer that afternoon and only said I'd go to dinner with him 'cause he said he'd sneak me into the writers' conference, and I hadn't read the fancy writers' books. Also, I didn't like being made fun of.

A little later, Algren asked, "Whatsa matter? You don't like your Cherries Jubilee?" and I, well, I picked up the bowl of whipped cream and smashed it in his face. Gasp, gasp. Czck, czck. Algren wiped his face, smiled, and said, "I was being kind of a jerk, wasn't I?" And then, "What'd you say your name was honey?" He gave me his phone number and said if I ever came to Chicago I should look him up.

Zahour insisted I read *City on the Make* and *Neon Wilderness*. I liked these books even better than the novels. I started thinking maybe Algren *was* a big deal. When we got to Chicago, I called him up, he gave me his address and asked me to dinner. I said, "I'm here with my boyfriend, could I bring him too?" Algren said, "No." So, I took the El by myself and somehow found his house on Evergreen.

We became friends when I moved here after college. He taught me to drink martinis. He also taught me to see the faces of faceless people living and working and lurking under the El. And to try to put my voice in harmony with their voices when I write. Sometimes I forget.

Zahour moved away. He called me the day Algren died. He was drunk and he was crying. I told him he was right about Algren, except the God part. But if God played poker, he'd sure ask Algren to the game.

I adapted *Neon Wilderness* and *City on the Make* into a musical. Regular playgoers came, but also old people with accents from Algren's old neighborhood. They said he would have liked it a lot.

"I stayed with my relatives on 61st Street, in the heart of the bustling South Side, where household names like Joe Louis, Sam Cook, Gale Sayers, Albertina Walker, and Ramsey Lewis, were all neighbors at one time or another."

JESSE JACKSON

God, I am in Chicago

I was born in Greenville, South Carolina, but came of age in Chicago. When I was a small child growing up in the South, we had an uncle who, many years before, had moved there —moved into a place at 61st and Vernon. All of us looked forward to the day we could join him. He would travel back home in the summertime to visit, and we'd stand there for hours waiting for his train to come in. After his stay, we went with him to the station and it was so sad when the train would pull off…how we desperately wanted to accompany him… bound for Chicago.

My first trip there came when I was about 15. My mother put me on a train leaving Greenville with some ham sandwiches, hard-boiled eggs, and potato pie. I rode up to Atlanta, where I transferred to the Hummingbird which went through Nashville and on into Chicago. I remember getting into the 63rd Street Station early on a Sunday morning. God, I was in Chicago. I went to the Lincoln Park Zoo, The Museum of Science and Industry, Comiskey Park—where I saw Billy Cox and Minnie Minoso; and to Wrigley Field, which, I thought, must be the most beautiful ballpark in all of America. There, I saw Gil Hodges, Jackie Robinson and Roy Campanella play. I stayed with my relatives on 61st Street, in the heart of the bustling South Side, where household names like Joe Louis, Sam Cook, Gale Sayers, Albertina Walker, and Ramsey Lewis, were all neighbors at one time or another.

At the Walgreens near 63rd and Cottage Grove, I could go and sit at the lunch counter, something I couldn't do down South. I saw blacks working behind the counter, and even black managers. I could see first-hand why there was so much romance attached to Chicago. It was one of the great, great watering holes for freedom, at least as we defined freedom in those days. I made a habit of visiting every summer.

In 1965, after finishing my undergraduate work, my wife and I moved to the city, into a home near 68th and Constance, as I began my studies at The Chicago Theological Seminary. Almost immediately, I became involved in the Chicago Coordinating Council of Community Organizations, and soon founded the Oakland Community Organization. My second year in Seminary, we went down to Selma, Alabama, because of the voting rights struggle there, and were part of the Bloody Sunday confrontation at the bridge. The following year, Martin

Luther King came to Chicago, and I began to work with him. My commitment was to civil rights and social justice all the while, but working with Dr. King magnified and strengthened that commitment many times over. Throughout that year, we tried to unveil Northern, urban racism, and show that it was just as vicious as Southern racism.

We picketed a very profitable chain of stores that operated in the black community because they steadfastly refused to hire black clerks, would not stock products produced by blacks, would not advertise in black newspapers, and would not put any money into black-owned banks. When the owners realized that they really had to become more responsive to their customers if they wanted to stay in business, the barriers started to come down. This method of confronting change through negotiation set the pace for the entire country. In the late '60s, much focus was on the models for social change that came out of Chicago.

Negotiating for change was an idea that endured. In early 1980, there had been a fire strike for 22 days, and 22 people had perished. A number of ministers asked if I would go and resolve it. I had no basis for feeling I could resolve it, but there existed a perception that I could. So I called Mayor Jane Byrne and asked her if I could help negotiate a settlement. She said I couldn't because the union representative was dishonorable. I went to the union rep and he said that I couldn't because the Mayor was dishonorable. I had to remind them both of the sad fact that, while they were busy calling each other names, people were dying.

In the meantime, black firemen were upset because white firemen were locking them out through the union process. Caught between the city and the union, black firemen were getting squeezed. Yet I felt that unionism and collective bargaining was worth fighting for—and racism worth fighting against. So I ended up meeting with the black firemen, the white fire union, and the city. After 48 hours of round-robin negotiations, on March 8, 1980, we brought the strike to a conclusion. It was a glorious moment because it involved Chicagoans coming together who had really never come together before. And many lives were saved.

Chicago, the city I moved to, was a very different place than the city I moved from more than two decades later. Not that it doesn't have a long way to go, just as the rest of the country does, but it has started along the path of becoming not just *my* kind of town, but truly *our* kind of town. A place where people, of all colors, can know each other a little better, talk to each other a little easier, and know with certainty that the city is theirs.

"The Mayor listened carefully without interrupting. When I was finished, he looked at me directly and asked, 'But what will it do for Chicago?'"

LEO MELAMED

What Will it Do for Chicago?

The 1990 Nobel Laureate in Economics, Merton Miller, nominated financial futures as "the most important financial innovation in the last two decades." At a minimum, this qualifies the International Monetary Market (IMM), the birthplace of financial futures, as a great Chicago story.

But back in 1975, long before Chicago's financial markets gained prominence, Mayor Richard J. Daley, the esteemed father of our city's present Mayor, knew this truth even without pedagogical credentials. Mayor Daley's support for our markets came at a critical early juncture in our history, at a time when it was much more difficult to divine the true promise of financial futures.

Indeed, when the IMM opened its doors in 1972 as a division of the Chicago Mercantile Exchange (CME), few outside of Chicago heralded the event as significant. To most observers of the financial scene, the opening of the IMM was not worthy of more than a passing comment. Precious few gave it any chance of success. Of course, the world misunderstood the potential and scope of the idea we spawned, and miscalculated the power of determined Chicagoans, particularly the members of the CME. Here is what I had to say in the IMM's first annual report, some six months after we began trading:

The opening of the International Monetary Market on May 16, 1972, was as revolutionary a step as the establishment of the first organized commodity exchange when that event occurred...we believe the IMM is larger in scope than currency futures alone, and accordingly, we hope to bring to our threshold many other contracts and commodities that relate directly to monetary matters and that would complement the economics of money futures.

Of course it was easier said than done. There was a sea of hatred and skepticism around us. Our idea was perceived as too revolutionary and Chicago was deemed the wrong locale. "It's ludicrous to think that foreign exchange can be entrusted to a bunch of pork belly crapshooters," proclaimed a prominent New York banker. "The New Currency Market: Strictly for Crapshooters," echoed *Business Week*.

Fortunately, there were some notable exceptions to the contemporary conventional wisdom, the most important of which came from another Nobel Laureate in Economics, Professor Milton Friedman. From the outset Professor Friedman, who held court at the University of Chicago, believed in our idea and became our most prominent champion. He gave us the credibility and courage to proceed. Indeed, without his unwavering support, the concept of financial futures might never have flourished and I would not be able to relate the following anecdote about the then-Mayor of our great city.

At the time of the IMM's birth, the CME was still housed in its 1927 location at Franklin and Washington. However, by 1969 it was obvious to me as Chairman that we had outgrown the premises. The trading floor had become far too small for the burgeoning business of futures and the bustling activities of its traders. Besides, I had some grandiose plans. So I called for a referendum, asking for authority from the members to build a new facility. It was a highly controversial proposal. Plans to move had been initiated on more than one occasion in the past but had always been defeated because any move was considered too risky.

Nevertheless, the referendum was held and approved by an overwhelming vote of 320 to 21. We were authorized to spend six million dollars, all we had in our treasury, to build a new building and construct a new trading floor. It was precious little money even by the standards of that day. Indeed, it was barely enough to build the glass structure and trading facility at 444 W. Jackson, just west of the Chicago River. But build it we did, and soon it provided us with a column-less 18,000 sq. ft. trading floor and an adjacent area for the necessary support facilities. It was the most modern market structure in the world. As a consequence, even though currency futures began life in the old quarters, we were confident that the new building would soon provide the IMM with room to expand.

Yet success had its price. The rapid growth of the IMM soon became a problem. In just three years from the date we moved, the allocated space for IMM contracts was insufficient. Worse yet, our ambitious plans for new financial markets in interest rates and stock indexes could not possibly be instituted within the four walls of the premises. We faced a terrible dilemma: To consider moving to new quarters in so short a time span was out of the question, but to stay as we were meant the end of IMM expansion. Our architects, Skidmore, Owings & Merrill, offered a bold solution. We could expand the building to the west by 90 feet, thereby increasing our trading area by 40 percent. It would solve all our immediate problems and allow us to proceed with all the new markets. But there was a terrible hitch. To carry out this plan we would need to purchase the air-rights from the City and cantilever the building over the Canal street sidewalk. Such an endeavor had been allowed only once in the history of Chicago and that was for a hospital. Our proposal was flatly rejected by Chicago's building department. If there was a chance that the plan could be realized, it would now take personal intervention by Mayor Richard J. Daley.

I was in my early thirties at the time and relatively unknown. To me, the Mayor was a godly figure whom I respected and revered. He was a man of international prominence, someone I read about in the press. Although I had been with him before, it had always been on festive occasions and was usually in the presence of others. But this time it would be different. This time it would be in his office on the fifth floor of City Hall, and this time I would be alone. I would be there not to offer the city assistance or to make an introduction, but to request a unique favor. I was terribly nervous and a little scared.

But I had come very prepared. I brought the architectural renderings and plans. I showed him the cost estimates. I explained the reason necessitating the action. The Mayor listened carefully without interrupting. When I was finished, he looked at me directly and asked, "But what will it do for Chicago?"

I wasn't really prepared for this question but I thought I knew the answer. "Mr. Mayor," I responded, "if I am right about financial futures, the IMM will move the center of gravity of U.S. finance a couple of feet westward from New York." The Mayor broke out into a wide smile. "I like that," he said with a chuckle, "go on and expand the building."

The rest is history. I guess Mayor Daley knew what Professor Miller later learned.

GWENDOLYN BROOKS, POET AND WRITER

21

It Is Good You Came

As you know, Harold Washington was a great reader. He had read much of my work. I really had met him only a time or two when he asked me to read a poem for the occasion of his first inauguration. I was so happy and proud to take part. When I went to the affair and it was my turn to speak, I came up to the podium and everyone in the room stood up; I don't know why. It was strange. This is the poem I read on that very special day in my life.

Mayor, world man, history man.
Beyond steps that occur and close
your steps are echo makers.
You can never be forgotten.

We begin our health
We enter the age of alliance

This is our senior adventure.

Well, it certainly was "our senior adventure," but not yet quite "the age of alliance" as we presently discovered. After I had read, I saw our new Mayor standing up and clapping with everyone else. It was a most delightful day for me.

When I got the news too few years later that Harold Washington had died I remember what a shock it was, as I guess it was for everybody. It seemed almost ridiculous that it could be happening. We all had so many hopes, because he seemed to be getting a grip on the affairs of the city. Too bad. I wrote this poem on the occasion of the Mayor's death and titled it, "The Last Inauguration of Harold Washington":

The time there was no time to anticipate
came anyhow.

Sleep, sleep.
Every hour was worth the tightening of purpose and vein.

You swept the city courtyard responsibly everyday.
You smiled and you waved everyday.
Everyday you charted, you chastened.

The circular ripples are riding, are reaching
beyond interrupting.

It is good you came.

HELMUT JAHN, ARCHITECT

22

Just as Planned

My original plan was to stay in Chicago for one year, do my thesis at the Illinois Institute of Technology, and return to Germany. But I stayed, initially, for the same reason architects stayed in this city a century before, a Chicago fire.

After I graduated from Technische Hochschule in Munich, I worked for P.C. von Seidlein for just over a year. Then, in 1966, I received a Rotary Scholarship to attend IIT and pursue graduate studies in architecture. At that time, Chicago was *the* mecca of modern architecture, and IIT was *the* school at which to learn it. I had planned, upon arrival, to begin my thesis work immediately, but because I hadn't done my undergraduate work at IIT, I was not allowed to proceed. There were members of the administration who assumed that I wasn't familiar with the essential principles—Miesian principles—and I was encouraged, in the meantime, to go out and find part-time employment.

I knew that I didn't want to work in a big office like Skidmore, Owings & Merrill, but rather, in a more intimate place, where I could really learn. I had made several acquaintances among my fellow graduate students, and one of them informed me that Gene Summers, one of Mies Van Der Rohe's three main collaborators, had just left to set up his own office. Gene was a figure with whom I was familiar through my German contacts, as well as through his actual work; he had designed the Berlin Museum, and had been instrumental in the design and execution of the Seagrams Building in New York. So I went to see Gene in late December of 1966, and after a little heckling over my salary, I joined his firm.

He had a nice office with about fifteen desks. Unfortunately, he had absolutely no work. He was doing a few rough studies for people he had known through Mies, including the Seagrams people, but we spent most of our time just talking about architecture, which taught me a great deal, and which we both seemed to enjoy.

It was on January 16, 1967, that everything changed in my life—the day that the original McCormick Place burned down. Gene lived in Hyde Park and had driven right by the fire on his way to work that day. He knew that McCormick Place was a total loss and that the entire structure would have to be rebuilt. Eventually, through a series of circumstances, Gene was contacted and invited to become a partner in the architectural firm of Charles Murphy in order to redesign and reconstruct the building. But it was not a move he considered light-ly. Though he wasn't as busy as he would have liked, there was something very satisfying about having his own shop, and he was beginning to establish a name for himself independent of his former collaborations. He did ask me my opinion, and I was quite positive about the chance to work on a project of such importance. When Gene finally accepted the offer to join Murphy, I came along as his right-hand man on the project. Consequently, I rarely went to school, and actually never did finish my thesis. Nor did I return to Germany after one year. As my first year in Chicago slipped by, I decided to stay a second year. Then I wanted to stay until McCormick Place was finished, and one thing after another until, more than 25 years later, I am still here.

If I remember back to my first few days in Chicago, it's surprising that I stayed. I was taking a leisurely swim off North Avenue Beach when I saw some people water-skiing—something which I had never seen. I swam out to their boat and asked if I could give it a try. They told me in so many words that I should take a hike. Despite this initial cool encounter, I've realized that I truly like Chicago and wouldn't want to live and work in another place. I have been spending more and more time in the past few years out of the country as our foreign commissions have increased, but Chicago is my home, I find it a very productive place to work and discern an attitude among the people that seems to get things done.

"We were two or three minutes into a tasteless scene about nuns and priests and sex. We definitely deserved to be booed off the stage."

GEORGE WENDT

Second Chance

People often ask why actors from *Second City* are so successful. Some say it's because of the audiences. Some say it's because the actors get the chance to write their own material, even "produce" and direct their own scenes. Some swear that it is the improvisational component—the trial by fire element—that ultimately produces solid actors. But I find that probably the most reasonable explanation for the success of *Second City* folks is just plain old *experience*. There are very few venues that give the opportunity of eight shows a week, 52 weeks a year, for, in some cases, a string of years. Most performers, if they're lucky, get in a show once or twice a year for a few weeks at a time. *Second City* crams an incredible amount of experience into a relatively short period of time.

I think that, for me, probably the most pronounced moment of hard-knocks experience was being booed off the stage at *Second City*, literally right off the stage. It happened back in 1976, during my first year in the resident company. There was nothing graceful about it at all. No sly rejoinders from me. No classic heckling put-downs. Just about six or seven people booing with all their might. That can make quite a racket in a house that only holds about 300 folks.

I was up on stage with three other players. I won't name them, but they were prominent *Second City* people. We were two or three minutes into a tasteless scene about nuns and priests and sex. We definitely deserved to be booed off the stage. At first, we tried the usual kinds of responses like, "Oooh those neighbors are noisy," or, "Oh Father, do you think that's the Holy Ghost?" We tried a few different ways to defuse it, but then it started to escalate beyond booing as they got more specific: "You're BORING people—Get off the stage—YOU'RE BORING!" I couldn't disagree with them. The lights flickered on and off uneasily. The poor stage manager must have been back there saying, "Should I bail on this? Yes! No! Yes!" There was no snappy blackout line, there was no soft, wonderful fadeout. There wasn't any dignity to it at all. Finally we were just standing there bewildered and dejected, and the lights came down for good. I walked off the stage, pulled off my gear and started walking directly to the exit of the theater, to go down the back stairs and onto Wells Street. I was really planning to walk out the door and never come back.

Our producer at the time, Bernie Sahlins, burst backstage and said, "Get back up there. You affected those people." Well, thank God he was there. He really tried to pump us up. I was mortified, humiliated, depressed. I wasn't even defiantly angry because I felt the hecklers were right. Ultimately, Bernie bolstered my confidence sufficiently in order for me to not leave show business. Now I think that every performer should be booed off the stage at least once, because it provides a real bedrock for your commitment to the theater, or show business in general. It's an experience all actors should have.

Looking back, I find myself wondering, who were those hecklers? Were they religious fanatics, or were they just discerning theater-goers? The point is I got their message. "I'll never do it again, Sister, I promise."

"Though I had been on the air in Chicago for over a year before *The Color Purple* was released, people outside of Chicago said, 'Isn't that nice, she got a talk show out of that.'"

OPRAH WINFREY

24

It Wasn't the Weather

Chicagoans love to talk about the weather. It's one of our favorite topics for good reason: It's serious enough to warrant conversation.

But the city's position on the weather map wasn't a factor in my decision to come here. In fact, I'd decided that Chicago was going to be my home even before I got a chance to experience its highs and lows myself. After seven years working as a reporter and anchorwoman in Baltimore, I decided that I was ready for a change, a new challenge. I knew I couldn't move to Washington, D.C., though it was only 40 miles away, after I learned that the ratio of eligible black men to women was so unpromising. And I knew I didn't want to move to New York because my trips there had always been too much, too hectic—too chaotic. After looking into a few other possibilities, my mind was made up. I was singing "Chicago, Chicago..." long before I had a job here.

On Labor Day weekend, 1983, Channel 7 flew me in for an audition. I didn't think I was going to get the job because, first of all, I was black and female, coming into a television market that was used to seeing faces that were white and male. Second of all, the city was starting to address a new layer of serious racial issues because Harold Washington, the city's first black mayor, had just been elected. But as I landed at O'Hare, I had this strange feeling that I was coming home and that this was the place where I would live and build my life. I *had* to find a job here.

I had planned to contact every other station in town if the job at Channel 7 didn't work out. But it turned out that on the very same day I auditioned, I was offered the job as host of a show called *A.M. Chicago*.

During my first year on the show, I was discovered for my role in the film, *The Color Purple*. The story goes that the producer, Quincy Jones, was passing through Chicago, and while staying at a hotel, saw me on TV. He had never even heard of me before, but decided to invite me to an audition. As everyone knows, I got the part, but very few know what the audition was really like.

It took place on what I still believe were the three coldest and windiest days in Chicago history. During the audition scene, for every step that I took I was blown back two. It was

OPRAH WINFREY, TELEVISION TALK SHOW HOST AND ACTRESS

so cold that my eyes were watering and the tears were instantly freezing on my cheeks. But like the character I was auditioning for, I was determined to make it. After two long months of waiting, I received the good news.

On the movie set, I remember I had a hard time convincing anyone I had a successful talk show in Chicago that was soon going to be broadcast nationally. When I mentioned it, most either reacted with an unimpressed, "That's nice, okay, now would you go stand over there please?" or assumed it was a late-night radio show. Not long after the movie was released, without my name even making the fine print on the poster, *Oprah* went national—and soon afterwards, they re-printed the poster with my name on it. (I'd tried to tell them it was going to be *big*.) Though I had been on the air in Chicago for over a year before *The Color Purple* was released, people outside of Chicago said, "Isn't that nice, she got a talk show out of that."

I have to say, though, good things have happened to me here. From the moment I arrived I just felt that the city embraced me, and I did the same in return. I wanted to give everyone a big hug.

They say that, if you can make it in New York, you can make it anywhere, but I think that phrase should belong to Chicago. When we went national, everybody wondered whether *Oprah* would be as well-received around the country, but I knew that we would be because we had *already* succeeded in Chicago; and Chicago, in my mind, represents the heart of America. This is where the real pulse of the country is. For the most part, Chicagoans aren't too strange or overwhelming and we rarely go off on tangents; instead, we're stable and consistent and we usually stay the course. Chicago's a *real* city in an era when so many others seem to be pretending.

"She vowed that if she had a son, she was going to name him after this great 'Jewish' martyr, Abraham Lincoln."

ABRAHAM LINCOLN MAROVITZ

25

My Son, Abraham

As I was growing up here in the city, I always heard stories about "self-made" men and women. Well, I'm not too short of 90 years and I have yet to meet one of them.

I know that I sure had a lot of help getting to where I am today. It started with my family. I was born to wonderful parents who, though they never had a day of schooling in their lives, brought with them from the Old Country a set of strong values which they inculcated into their children's young hearts. As the five of us would leave for school each morning, my mother would kiss us and remind us to do our little "mitzvah" for the day, our "good deed." I gradually realized the importance of these mitzvahs and was lucky enough to be on the receiving end of quite a few of them.

As a youngster, we lived next door to a boxer named King Rollo, a sparring partner of the former World Heavyweight Champion, John L. Sullivan. King taught me what he knew and by the time I was 16 and had finished high school, I was a pretty good boxer, fighting in many tournaments and stags where I picked up a few dollars. At about the same time, I landed a job at Mayer, Meyer, Austrian, and Platt, then the largest law firm in Chicago, as an office boy for $10 a week. I hadn't been on the job for more than a few weeks when I showed up with a cut eye and a cut lip. "What the hell happened to you?" my boss, Mr. Austrian, inquired. I told him I was a boxer and that, though I had faced a tough opponent the previous night, a stocky worker from one of Gary's steel mills, I had got the decision. "So you want to be a prize fighter?" he questioned further. I told him that I honestly didn't know what I wanted to be. "Get over to Kent College and start earning your law degree," he ordered. In those days all you needed was a high school diploma and, of course, tuition money. I did as I was told, even though I knew there wasn't a chance that I would be able to afford it. Mr. Austrian sent for me the following day and I reported to him that the tuition for one year was $120, and that I couldn't even spare 120 cents because my family needed the ten bucks I was earning each week. Upon hearing this, he called in the cashier at the firm, Elmer Enquist, and instructed him to start paying me $12 a week and to make out a check for the whole year's tuition. Mr. Austrian then told me that I could consider it a loan which I could pay back at $2 a week—money which he never took from me. Mr. Austrian took me

ABRAHAM LINCOLN MAROVITZ, SENIOR FEDERAL JUDGE

under his wing and helped me make my first steps toward a career, just as, a few years later, Alderman Jack Arvey, of the 24th Ward, took me under his political wing and was responsible for my election to the Illinois State Senate. The good alderman's efforts helped me become, in 1938, the first member of the Orthodox Jewish religion to be elected to that distinguished body. As I think back about my career and my life, and consider the phrase "self-made," I know that it doesn't apply to me. I think that what makes this city and this country great is the existence of people who are always ready to help others, always ready to give others a chance.

One of these people who always did seem ready, and someone with whom I felt a strong kinship, was a man elected to the State Senate the same year I was: Richard J. Daley. One of the first questions he asked upon making my acquaintance was how a nice Jewish fella wound up with the name "Abraham Lincoln." I'll tell you the same true story I told him. My mother had four brothers and a sister. All four brothers left Lithuania before the turn of the century; the oldest brother went to New York. After the death of my mother's mother, he sent for my Ma and her younger sister, who were 15 and 13 years of age respectively, to join him in New York. Upon their arrival, he found my mother a job in one of the infamous sweatshops of turn-of-the-century New York. She worked long hours for very little money. He also enrolled her in a settlement house sponsored by two rich Jewish German bankers, the Strauss brothers, where she was taught about the customs and the language of her new country. She was a religious woman, and one of the things she learned was that the German Jews called their synagogues, "temples." She also heard a lecture about Samuel Gompers, an English Jew who founded the American Federation of Labor. And then she heard a lecture about our great sixteenth president. During the lecture, they showed the class a picture of Abraham Lincoln with a beard, and sadly explained that he had been shot in the "temple." In Mother's mind, she concluded that Abraham Lincoln was a German Jew who had been shot in the synagogue. She vowed that if she had a son, she was going to name him after this great "Jewish" martyr, Abraham Lincoln. After she moved to Chicago, met and married my father and started to have a family, she was able to do just that.

Now, although usually Orthodox Jews name their children after deceased relatives, my mother wanted to name my brother, who appeared on the scene two years before I did,

"Abraham Lincoln." But my Pa said that there wasn't anybody yet named after his father, and my Ma couldn't quarrel with that. But when my paternal grandmother came to stay with the family in the final months of my mother's pregnancy with me, she asked my Ma if she would name her child, if it was a boy, after her father, "Abraham." (My grandma later said she had asked with reluctance because she had been turned down by her own four daughters.) Mother just smiled and said that she would. So when I was born, she named me Abraham Lincoln, and that is what my birth certificate shows.

I think that those of us who have been as lucky as I have been have an obligation to the community to pass off some of this good luck that we've had to others. I may sound like a big cornball or a big ham, but the day is lost for me if, at the end of the day, I can't think of some little thing that I did to help someone not as lucky as I.

ANCHEE MIN, WRITER AND ARTIST

Thoughts for My Daughter

Lauryan was born in Chicago at St. Anthony's Hospital on October 8, 1991. It was the moment I felt I really took root in this country. I remember my heart screamed in joy, "She is an American! My daughter is an American!"

I felt proud, safe and peaceful. No one in my family, including myself, thought that I could make it this far when I started the process of coming to America back in 1983.

That was a time when I had worked for the Shanghai Film Studio for six years as a janitor. I was treated like a machine. I had tuberculosis but was not allowed to take any leave. I was given assignment after assignment, south to Canton, north to the China-Russian border, west to Yunnan Province. Completely exhausted, I could see no end to my misery. I collapsed, passed out on the sets many times, and coughed blood. Sympathetic to my situation was my friend, Joan Chen, who at the time was in California. When she wrote and suggested that I try to come to America, for me it was like finding a light in hell. I lost sleep over the idea.

I could hardly imagine myself being in a land of which I had no knowledge. I spoke no English. I had nothing but guts. Joan helped me get into the School of the Art Institute of Chicago, the only school in the United States that would accept me based solely on my painting portfolio, and not also on an English proficiency exam.

I was desperate and my whole family became involved in my battle for a new life. Everyday we lived in a sweet dream, scared that any moment bad news would wake us up. My father looked out of the window constantly waiting for the mailman to deliver the passport. My mother stared at the tips of my chopsticks when I ate—she was lost in her worry over me. Finally my passport came. But my father's worry deepened. We all knew going to the U.S. Consulate to apply for a visa was the hardest obstacle to overcome. Many young people tried and got rejected for no apparent reason. I was 26 years old, had no school degrees and had many other disadvantages. But I was determined to "Hit my head on the southern wall until it bled"—only then would I stop. I borrowed my mother's white shirt and green skirt to wear for good luck on the day I went to the U.S. Consulate for a visa. Mother saw me off by the lane and said that she worried that the consul was going to find out that I didn't speak English. I told her that he would have no chance to find out because I had prepared to recite large paragraphs of self-introduction in the consul's face. I'd make him think my English was fluent.

A miracle happened. I was granted a visa. The translator at the consulate later told me that the consul-general liked my determination. I cried when I stepped out of the consulate gate. It was the happiest moment in my life.

When I got home my father and mother's face were deadly pale. Staring at me, holding their breath, they were not able to bring themselves to ask, "Did you get it?" They were afraid that I would say, "no." I took out the passport and showed them the red-green visa stamp. Letting out a huge breath, my father lost his strength. He almost fell on his knees. He struck my shoulders, and said loudly, "My monkey daughter, I can't believe this! Our ancestors are going to be proud of you. I am, because it's my character you inherited."

My mother stood aside, smiling. I hadn't seen my mother looking so happy for years. She was wiping off her running tears. I said "Mama, it was your clothes that brought me luck!" "No, it's love," replied mother, "it's love and faith."

Ten years have passed. I have been a happy Chicagoan—in love with the city. I learned my beginning English at a language school at University of Illinois, and by watching Channel 11 children's programs; I've worked a dozen jobs, as a waitress, gallery attendant, messenger, babysitter, painter, photographer. It was not easy, but for the first time I worked for myself and was treated as a human being. I remember my first winter in Chicago. I was too poor to afford public transportation, so I bought a used bicycle and rode to the school everyday, sometimes with the weather below zero. Although it was freezing cold, my heart was warm. When I passed downtown I often said to myself, "All right, that is the Sears Tower! I see it, I am not dreaming, I am in Chicago, Illinois, U.S.A.

I miss my family in China but I know they are happy for me. It makes me feel wonderful to know that my daughter is an American. To me, being an American means having the right to work toward one's happiness. I hope Lauryan will appreciate this country the way I do. I was a rice-shoot in a drought season. I appreciate every drop of rain by heart.

On Christmas Day, Lauryan came to me with a piece of chocolate in her hand and asked me what it was. She is as strong as a little bear. I have tried to teach her to do without sweets, but it's hard to deny her. At her age, I was starving. Now I have to pinch myself daily, because we have plenty in the land of plenty—my dream. My dream for her.

I plan to take Lauryan to China every year and teach her Chinese. I think it is important that she is made to be aware of how different life could have been for her.

KOKO TAYLOR, BLUES SINGER

27

Making Records

Igrew up singing blues and gospel because every Sunday, without fail, my family went to church. My daddy used to say that everybody in his household had to go—he didn't care what the kids did on the other days of the week, but on Sunday, we had to be in church—so that's where I was. But I loved singing anyway. I used to listen to the radio and get inspiration from people like Bessie Smith, Muddy Waters, Jimmy Reed, Sonny Boy Williamson, Big Momma Thornton—folks like that. The more I listened, the more I got into it. Music became the soul of my life.

When I got a little older and had moved up to Chicago, I used to be part of jam sessions with friends and acquaintances in little clubs on the South Side, and it wasn't for the money. None of us needed to be paid for those kinds of sessions. I'd get up and sing, and some of the other women would join in, like Big Time Sarah and Zora Young. Different musicians were there at different times. Guys like Lonnie Brooks, Son Seals, Buddy Guy, Junior Wells, Johnny Shines, and Sunnyland Slim, there on the piano. You couldn't have bought the fun we were having. Some of the sessions went on and on, late into the night, and on into the morning. It wasn't unusual for the sun to be rising above the lake by the time we were going home.

In the early days of my career, I didn't have an official booking agency or manager. The late great Willie Dixon came the closest to filling that role. After Willie heard me one night in 1963, casually sitting in with the Howlin' Wolf Band and Muddy Waters in one of those little clubs, he came over to me and said, "My God, I ain't never heard a woman sing the blues like you do. Where in the world did you come from?" He asked if I had recorded with anybody, and, at that time, I didn't even know what "to record" with somebody meant. "How would you like to make a record?" he asked. I told him okay, but I honestly didn't know if I should be all that excited. He brought me over to Chess Records, on South Michigan Avenue, where he recorded and produced for a variety of people. He wrote my first song and I recorded it for Chess. That was how I started working with Willie Dixon. We stuck together over the years, writing and singing, right up until he died.

The first North Side club I ever sang in was *Wise Fool's Pub*, in 1971. It's hard to believe looking back, but before that year, you couldn't hear hardly any blues at all on that side of town. I sang with an older black man named Johnny. He used to play an instrument that looked like a little banjo—almost like a guitar, only miniature. Everybody seemed to love us. I know that some of the people that came in there were a little surprised because they weren't used to hearing that kind of music, but as new as it was to them, it was also new to us. We didn't know what to expect, facing white audiences who were unfamiliar with blues, especially when compared to our black audiences, who grew up with it. Before long, though, blues proved it had universal appeal. Blues clubs were soon opening up like popcorn, all over the city; *Biddy Mulligan's, Kingston Mines, B.L.U.E.S.*

These days, the blues have gone well beyond the South Side, beyond the city limits, beyond any limits at all; it's popular all over the world. Most months of the year, I'm on the road, working. Even in Europe, people come out in big numbers to hear me. I've been hanging in there now for about 30 years and I ain't tired yet. I still love traveling, making new fans and singing the blues.

"On television I saw my old high school classmate, Bill Murray, as a *Not-Ready-For-Prime-Time-Player*. I had seen him in the school auditorium as Professor Harold Hill in *Music Man* when he was a skinny little pimply-faced kid."

WILLIAM PETERSEN

28

Beef Stew

Iran away from home when I was 15 and headed down to the Loop, not knowing exactly where I would end up or what I was going to do. I wandered into one of the massive old theaters at Randolph and State, where they were running Clint Eastwood Westerns around the clock and spent the whole day in the balcony trying to figure out my next step. After 12 hours of watching the monumental image of Clint with his serape and weathered hat, the answer was clear—head west and become a cowboy. I walked a few blocks to the Greyhound Station and bought a ticket to Denver.

When the bus pulled into Denver, it dawned on me that it wasn't going to be easy for a 15-year-old in a strange city to get a job. So, instead of trying to find employment, I headed for the nearest movie theater. *Butch Cassidy and the Sundance Kid* happened to be playing. I wanted to be what I saw on the screen—a cowboy, a bandit, a railroad man, a drifter—I watched the movie three times before I decided it was time to move on. Salt Lake City sounded good to me.

But I didn't last long in the Beehive State. A construction company turned me down flat when I asked for a job. I looked like a kid. That night, just after midnight, a real cowboy with a six-pack of beer invited himself into my flophouse room. After just a day, I'd had enough. My last few dollars were spent on bus fare to my brother's place in Idaho.

I stayed in Idaho for seven years, finishing high school, pumping gas, going to college, serving as youth coordinator for Bud Davis' narrowly missed 1972 U.S. Senate bid, working as a stagehand, taking acting classes, being in plays, getting married, having a daughter, becoming a logger, working at a newspaper. At some point, I started to hear rumblings about Chicago theater and the great work they were doing. On television, I saw my old high school classmate, Bill Murray, as a *Not-Ready-For-Prime-Time-Player*. I had seen him in the school auditorium as Professor Harold Hill in *Music Man* when he was a skinny little pimply-faced kid. My friends and I had mocked the hell out of this guy, even while admitting privately that he looked like he was having fun.

I'd heard and seen as much as I needed to. I packed up our few belongings in a rented U-Haul, and we made our way back to Chicago. Within 36 hours of making the city limits,

I auditioned and was cast in a small Off-Loop production. I was hungry.

What I wandered into was an explosion of creative talent. The Chicago theater community in the mid '70s was not only starting to do ground-breaking work that was locally appreciated, it was starting to receive national attention, shaking up the theater world. I got even more excited when I realized there were people who actually made a living in the theater. After my initial success, I didn't work for a year; I was becoming an actor, while being a waiter. But things were happening. I took classes and workshops at *Victory Gardens*, eventually getting my actor's card there. I was hanging out with David Mamet, Joe Mantegna, Laurie Metcalfe, Elizabeth Perkins, Joanie Allen, Gary Cole. *Steppenwolf* was just starting. Jimmy Belushi was doing "Sexual Perversity in Chicago." Anything was possible.

So many of us have gone on to be successful in Hollywood; we get together and can't figure out how the hell it happened. But, for me anyway, if L.A. represents nouvelle cuisine and a fancy night out, Chicago represents a nice beef stew and a home-cooked meal.

You never forget where you come from when you're from Chicago. I remember getting back into town after finishing *To Live and Die in L.A.* during which I had been treated like the big tuna. I dropped by to say hi to everyone at *Remains*, and within two minutes, they had me up on a ladder with a paint roller. There was plenty of work to be done. It felt good to be home.

" Years later, I related this story to Judy Belushi and she remembered the night John came back from the *Harper Theater*, stunned. John told her, 'Gee, I got thrown out of there. They said I stole twenty bucks.'"

JOYCE SLOANE

JOYCE SLOANE, PRODUCER EMERITUS OF THE SECOND CITY

29

Earth Mother

They call me Earth Mother. I'm the doting figure behind the scenes at *Second City* helping to get things done. It's a good thing, because no matter who's on stage improvising, there's always just as much work out of the spotlight, including the recruitment of talent. Of all our alumni, I am most often asked how John Belushi was discovered, and interestingly, his story is the most vague.

In the late '60s, one of my many jobs here was to promote *Second City's* underground, experimental film program for Bell & Howell into area colleges. One day, I went to the College of DuPage where I met with the Director of Student Activities. I gave him my speech about how young directors were challenging the film establishment and that the public would no longer be satisfied with predictable plots and camera angles. I also started to tell him about another program we offered, the *Second City Touring Company*, which could perform our latest show right on campus. "No thanks," he said, "we've seen it. We have a student who goes to see all your shows, then comes back and does the whole thing for us." "Really? I'd like to meet this guy," I said coolly, thinking that, very possibly, I was wasting my whole day out in DuPage County. "Well, as a matter of fact, he's right over there." There he was, playing foosball; my first memory of John Belushi. We walked over and the Director said, "John, this is so and so from *Second City*, she's interested in talking to you." I remember how John looked up at me with one raised eyebrow…the rest, as they say, is history.

However, John swore to me that our first meeting occurred under completely different circumstances. He claimed that, back when *Second City* cast members did improvs at the *Harper Theater* in Hyde Park, I had thrown him out after accusing him of stealing $20 from the lobby coffee shop, which was run by a guy named Shebaba. I never believed John, and have no recollection of that happening, but he even knew the manager's name!

Years later, I related this story to Judy Belushi and she remembered the night John came back from the *Harper Theater*, stunned. John told her, "Gee, I got thrown out of there. They said I stole twenty bucks." I told Judy I never did that, but apparently John insisted that I had. I guess in the end, it's not that important how John was discovered, but how deeply he touched all of us, that matters most.

JOSEPH CARDINAL BERNARDIN, ARCHBISHOP

In Partnership

I came to Chicago as a stranger. And even though I had heard a great deal about the city and had visited a number of times, I was really overwhelmed by its size and complexity. I came from Cincinnati, which was a much smaller and more homogenous community. Here, the sheer size of the area, but in particular, the size of the Archdiocese—the number of parishes, schools, priests and parishioners—was almost overwhelming. As was its diversity. Every weekend in Chicago, we celebrate Mass in some 19 or 20 languages. As I go around to the different parishes, I sometimes feel as though I'm presiding over different Churches. The liturgy celebrated in the African-American community, for example, is quite different, in terms of the music and the style of preaching, from the liturgy celebrated in the Polish-American, Hispanic, or Asian-American communities. And yet, despite all the diversity, there really is a unity because we belong to one Church, all committed to the Catholic faith. That was really what impressed me most when I first came here.

I have been in Chicago for more than a decade now and have been very much at home here, and much involved in the life of the Catholic Church, as well as the life of the community. And I've had some wonderful experiences. One particular trait or quality of Chicago that comes to mind is that of partnership; when there is a problem that needs to be resolved or an issue that needs to be addressed, people are willing to work with each other. I'd like to give several examples of the effectiveness of partnership that come to mind.

The Catholic Church has well over 100 schools with 42,000 students in the inner-city of Chicago. These schools are serving people who are poor, marginalized. Eighty percent or more are minority students; at least 40 percent are not Catholic. These students want to go to our schools because we give a quality education and we teach values. But it's very difficult for us to maintain the schools because of the cost. We don't want to charge too much tuition, because the families who send their children to our schools don't have much to spare. The Archdiocese spends a considerable amount of its own resources, but it's not enough. So, seven years ago, I started the Big Shoulders Fund, to ask the broader community, especially corporations and foundations, as well as interested individuals, to assist with our inner-city schools. I made it very clear that we were not in competition with the public schools; the well-being of this city depends upon good schools, both public and private.

The response was tremendous. In the seven years that Big Shoulders has been in existence, we have raised over 35 million dollars. And that money has come from Catholics, Jews, and Protestants—people who are committed to the well-being of the city and know the importance of a good education. I think the Big Shoulders Fund is a wonderful example of the kind of partnership that we have developed between the Church and the broader community, a partnership that has provided quality education to a significant number of young people in this city.

A similar kind of partnership exists within the Church itself, we call it our Sharing Program. We have many parishes in poorer sections of the city which don't have enough resources of their own to keep going and to fully fund their schools. So the more affluent parishes will "adopt" a poor parish and share with it not only money, but other things as well. For example, they visit each other; each going to the other's liturgy or social affair. This really has established wonderful bonds between people of different ethnic, racial and economic backgrounds. People seldom hear about this sharing. Certainly the public-at-large does not know very much about it, but each year, the sharing goes on among the people of most of our nearly 400 parishes.

I also want to mention Catholic Charities, another example of tremendous partnership. Each year Catholic Charities touches the lives of over half a million people of all ethnic backgrounds, races and religions in Cook and Lake Counties. Catholic Charities tries to respond to whoever is in need. But where do we get the resources? Many people, both Catholic and non-Catholic, give money or volunteer their time. Catholic Charities also cooperates with various government agencies, especially in responding to the needs of children and the elderly. On the North Side, for example, we have the Maryville-Columbus Reception Center, where we care for hundreds of cocaine babies. The resources for that, in large part, come from public funding. But there are also hundreds of volunteers who help take care of these babies. The basic treatment is to cuddle these babies, and we have men and women who come from all over the city to give their time. Catholic Charities is a great multi-dimensional partnership that makes it possible for the Church to reach out to people in need.

I don't want to give the impression, however, that all of our problems are resolved, or that all the serious issues have been addressed. We still have mammoth problems to confront—problems which are negatively affecting the well-being of our community. It will only be through a real determination to address these problems collaboratively that we will succeed in the long run. Success will only come if we work together in a real partnership. Both the Big Shoulders Fund and Catholic Charities are evidence of the willingness of the people of the Chicago area to work with the Church. This gives me much satisfaction and I am deeply grateful.

Innocence in Chicago

I graduated from being a kid when at the age of ten I discovered that, between the bus system and the El, I could go anywhere in the city. I was raised to have a strong level of independence, and soon I did. My family lived on the North Side on a little street called Hutchinson where my best and only friend, Kathleen Coleman, lived across the street. We used to save our allowances to finance our weekend adventures, most often making the trip to The Museum of Science and Industry. Just the idea of eating a doughnut that tasted like mashed potatoes, or sharing quiet secrets in the whisper chamber, was enough to get us out of our houses and onto the bus for the long ride south.

The coal mine at the museum was where we used to go for a thrill. The cool, dark place was kind of creepy for two little girls, but it was a place that brought out that sense of adventure we seemed to be searching for. We hadn't made the trip to the museum too many times before we were devising elaborately detailed plans to hide out there overnight, being careful to avoid not only the night guard but also the areas we thought were just too scary. The endless stretches of uncharted space within the building fascinated us, and the more time we spent there, the more we felt at home, like somehow we belonged there.

One of the reasons that we felt so completely at home there was logical: Kathleen's grandmother had a replica of the huge, intricate dollhouse that was permanently on display in the basement of the museum. Her relative had made the original. Kathleen's wasn't an exact replica, but it was close enough to make us feel that we had more than just a passing sense of familiarity with each of its more than 100 rooms.

It was an innocent time for me growing up, unaware that any of the world's dangers or problems existed. As I think back about growing up on a quiet street in the middle of Chicago, it's as if I was living in the realm of Scout in *To Kill A Mockingbird*. I am surprised that I was as naive as I was, shocked at discovering the inequity and prejudice that exists in the real world.

Someone must have watched over me until I was old enough to watch over myself. I just haven't figured out who that might have been.

Chicago Beat

Should I get serious and discuss politics? I could tell you about the days when Harry Truman was president. He was a very dear friend and I had wide access to the White House in those days. One thing that President Truman tipped me on in 1952 soon became national news. Adlai Stevenson was going to be the next Democratic candidate for president. Adlai was trying to avoid running because he wanted to distance himself from Truman, whose popularity was at low ebb. History has been kind to Truman in the intervening years and he now is recognized as a great president. At that time, however, he wasn't winning high percentages in any opinion polls. Truman told me how he had to sit Adlai down and talk to him like a Dutch uncle, telling him he had no choice but to be the candidate. Of course, Stevenson went on to head the Democratic ticket. Unfortunately, he ran twice and was defeated twice. He was a remarkable man, though, and someone who would have brought a lot of intelligence and dynamism to the White House.

But the subject of politics doesn't appeal to everybody—maybe I should tell you a few of the many stories that grew out of my 27 years hosting *Kup's Show*. We had countless figures of national and international prominence on the interview program, including Richard Nixon, Jimmy Carter, Robert McNamara, Martin Luther King, Margaret Mead, Norman Rockwell, Edward R. Murrow, William F. Buckley, Truman Capote, Muhammad Ali, Bob Hope, Bette Davis, Marlon Brando, Audrey Hepburn, Robert Redford... Sometimes we invited particular guests to provide counterpoints for each other, but I never could predict exactly what would happen.

One night we had Jimmy Hoffa, the late labor leader, who was a man far more intelligent than people gave him credit for, pitted against Mortimer Adler, one of the country's great intellects. Hoffa just demolished him. Jimmy talked straight to the common man without fancy language, and got right down to the heart of what people wanted to hear. Poor Mortimer barely opened his mouth before he lost the audience; his refined arguments were just beyond most people's comprehension. Consequently, Jimmy Hoffa came off brilliantly against Mortimer Adler. Television has a mysterious way of allowing some people to shine, while others are rendered less than they are in real life. One night, we had the four

IRV KUPCINET, JOURNALIST

Eisenhower brothers on, including the former president. And though Dwight Eisenhower was once the most powerful man in the nation, if not the world, his brother Milton, who was a college president at the time, appeared far more intelligent and articulate than his renowned brother. Like I said, you never knew what would happen.

But maybe I should limit myself to the subject of sports. That would narrow my focus and help me maintain some cohesion—I started out as a sportswriter, after all. Maybe I should go all the way back to the days when I was officiating in the National Football League and was selected as one of the four officials for the Bears 1940 Championship game against the Washington Redskins. The two best and meanest teams in the league, going head to head. The day the invincible Bears scored 73 points while the Redskins didn't even get on the board. A tough game for Washington and a tough game for the officials, who had to run up and down the field as many times as the players. Towards the end of the game we were told to discourage the Bears from kicking any more extra points because they were running out of footballs. "Tell the Bears either to run the ball in, or pass it in. Just don't send another ball into the stands." One of the great highlights of my so-called sports career.

George Halas, the legendary Bears coach, was known to take great delight in screaming at the officials, berating them with the vilest language known to man when he felt a decision went against his team. I was, myself, subject to his rantings. Yet after many games, we sat down to dinner together, without even a word passing between us about our encounters on the field. As far as Halas was concerned, his hostility ended with the game.

Halas used to tell a story about me and my officiating skills that he never would admit was apocryphal; he told it so many times, he started to believe it. Seems Chicago was playing its bitterest rival, Green Bay, at Green Bay, and I was the headlinesman for the day. It was the usual ferocious match between the Bears and the Packers. Late in the game the Bears were marching for the winning touchdown and reached the Packers' 10-yard line. It was fourth and one, when Sid Luckman handed off to Bill Osmanski for an off-tackle dive, desperately trying for the first down. It was close. Too close to call. As headlinesman, I had to handle the measurement, and when I saw that the Bears made it, Halas said that I jumped up and down, clapped my hands over my head, and screamed, "We made it! We made it!" The Green Bay coach, Curly Lambeau, Halas said, was so incensed that he demanded the

League fire me immediately.

I want to assure one and all that the tale George Halas loved to tell was indeed apocryphal, but I have to say that it contained an underlying truth. I have an enduring love for the city in which I've spent more than 80 years. And I'm always ready to do whatever it takes.

SID LUCKMAN, HALL OF FAME CHICAGO BEARS QUARTERBACK

33

More than Money

George Halas hated the word *I*. With him, it was always *we*. After we had annihilated the Redskins in the infamous 73-0 rout for the 1940 World Championship, I wanted to meet with Coach Halas to discuss the possibility of some kind of bonus. I had talked about the question of whether or not I deserved a bonus with my family and friends and had concluded that, even though I was getting paid $5,000 a year and was probably one of the most well-paid players in the league, we had just had a terrific year and terrific game and that a bonus of $1,000 wasn't out of the question.

I went to Halas' office and asked him straight out. He just looked at me. I looked back at the man who was the Bears' founder, owner, coach, general manager, and treasurer, and saw him turn white. But as he regained his composure, he pulled an envelope out of a pocket and started reading his scribblings on its backside: "In the first game against Green Bay you threw an interception…" "But Coach," I interrupted, "we won that game by 30 points!" "…in the next game against Detroit you fumbled…" "But Coach, we beat the Lions by a wide margin! I must have done something right because I played 55 minutes in both of those games, on offense and defense!" It was no use. He went on and on, listing chronologically all of the lousy plays I had made that season. Finally I said, "Jeez, Coach, maybe I should pay you some money for as bad as it sounds like I've played." Coach Halas eyed me and told me he'd give me $250—and that it was more than I deserved and more than he wanted to pay me. I told him that I would never try to negotiate another contract with him. I told him to pay me what he wanted, because I didn't want anything to interfere with the admiration, love and respect I had for him. We shook hands and agreed.

I drove home to New York where I had grown up and where I was living during the off-season. Sometime in April, he wrote me a wonderful letter in which he stated that many things were going to change with the Bears' offense that coming year, and he suggested that I come back a month earlier than planned. If I did, he would pay me $750. I wrote him a letter back telling him that I was so interested in his idea that I would come back two months early for $1,500. He called me on the phone and we shared a good laugh. He said, "Listen to me: it's one month, get out here, we have a lot of work to do." So I ended up getting the bonus after all. He just had to arrange it his way.

He was right about the amount of work, we were up day and night and I loved it. By working on Coach Halas' new T-formation, I felt part of one of the greatest eras in the history of the sport. We truly revolutionized football, so much so that before too long, there wasn't a high school, college, semi-pro, or pro team that didn't utilize a T-formation offense.

As I think back about all of the spectacular games the Bears played, especially during the years that we dominated the sport, winning four World Championships in six years, one game stands out: The 1943 Championship game against the Washington Redskins and their quarterback, the great "Slinging Sammy" Baugh. It was one of the great highlights of my life and the best game ever for the Chicago Bears, George Halas, and Sid Luckman. The whole team was psyched up for a great victory and every member, including Bronko Nagurski, Dante Magnani, and Bulldog Turner, did their share. I had the thrill of throwing five touch-down passes, being the leading ground-gainer, and intercepting three Redskins passes while on defense, on the way to a 41-21 victory. A great day for Chicago and the Bears.

As a Chicago Bear under George Halas, I had the most thrilling experiences anyone could ever have—and nobody can ever take that away.

"Before Marina City, the tallest concrete structure we'd ever built was maybe seven stories but we figured, hell, if we can do seven, we can do sixty."

JAMES McHUGH

Impossible

I think there are certain things that can only happen in Chicago. There's a drive, a spirit you don't see anywhere else. Marina City embodied that.

When we were first approached about doing the job back in 1960, I had just become president of the company. Needless to say, I felt some trepidation, but the opportunity was very intriguing and exciting, not only to me but to the other people in the company. At the time, nothing like that building existed in the world. A lot of people across the country looked at the design and said, "Forget it. It's impossible." When I first saw the drawings I didn't know if it was pie-in-the-sky or what. After a while, though, it became apparent that the developers really meant to build this thing, and we decided that if they were mad enough to do it, we were crazy enough to be the ones to put it up. It was a risk—accepting the project—but that's always been the kind of job we like. There's a lot of satisfaction in finding a way to do the undoable.

It took a lot of innovation to construct Marina City. There were so many things that had never been done before. There had never been a way to make the sculptured concrete that created the corncob effect, so we developed a type of fiberglass mold that's a standard today. This was the first time anyone ever used a climbing crane in this country. Today, you don't see a high-rise project without them. It was the first time a high-rise building used all electric heat. There had never been a concrete building that tall anywhere. Before Marina City, the tallest concrete structure we'd ever built was maybe seven stories but we figured, hell, if we can do seven, we can do sixty.

It was a special time in Chicago. There was a feeling that you could do anything if you set your mind to it, and the city would support you. I think the people behind Marina City personified that—Bill McFettridge, Charles Swibel and Bertrand Goldberg, the architect. They were pretty strong personalities, but we came to a consensus that we were going to get these buildings done, and the only way to do it was by working together. That feeling showed up at every level, too. At the time, there was considerable acrimony between the carpenters and the ironworkers, but at Marina City they set that aside. They might beat the tar out of each other after working hours, but when they came back they were all on the same side because there was so much enthusiasm for this project.

We knew Marina City was something special, but we were really surprised by the international outpouring of admiration and recognition for the building. Even now, when people from other countries visit Chicago, they know Marina City. It's still a thrill to drive past the building or see it in the architecture books and say, "We did that."

Chicago has always been an impressive town for architecture, but Marina City touched off a new golden age. It set the stage for a whole series of structures that accomplished the impossible: the John Hancock Building, Sears Tower, Water Tower Place.

Historically, Chicago has been a city that loves to attempt the untried. Its civic voice says, "We are going to do things differently." Marina City really validated that spirit. It said to the people who build cities, "What you are doing so far is mediocre. We're going to go out and do something extraordinary." And you still see that unique Chicago attitude today.

"The first question I usually ask is 'Are you really from Chicago or did you grow up in Schaumburg?'"

AMY MADIGAN

Not From Schaumburg

My mother and father were pretty liberal when that was an extremely unpopular way to be in our neighborhood. They encouraged me to read what I wanted to read, see the films I wanted to see, dress how I wanted to dress. In essence, they taught me to think for myself. My dad was news director at Chicago's CBS-owned TV station so we usually had four televisions going at once, while he kept an eye on the competition. I felt very alive in that environment. In school, I was in all of the speech contests, all the piano competitions, involved in all the sports and in all the plays. From a very early age, I knew that I wanted to be a performer.

I grew up in South Shore, right by the lake, in the epitome of a city neighborhood. I felt connected to it in a visceral way. Every day, I walked to school, a Catholic school that I attended with all sorts of kids—Irish like myself, black kids, Hispanic kids. During that time, I learned several important things: I learned about being with different kinds of people, I learned a genuine love of literature, and I learned that it was okay for me to get up in front of people and perform—a daring step because it required a certain amount of arrogance.

From serious piano lessons with Sister Cecelia Mary, as a kid, I went on to play in a number of rhythm and blues bands during and after college, traveling around and working seven nights a week. But soon, I took the energy I had been putting into music and put it into acting; a choice that has taken me all over the country and put me in touch with many different people.

It's always fun to meet a fellow Chicagoan. It's like blood. The first question I usually ask is "Are you really from Chicago or did you grow up in Schaumburg?" There is a difference. If it turns out that they're really from Chicago, I get into a healthy debate about our respective neighborhoods. I always win, though, because my neighborhood was without peer. We even had a cheer, "Say it with reverence, say it with pride, Chicago's great South Side!"

I get back here as often as I can because it's where my family and so many friends are. It reminds me that I was brought up to know what *family* and *home* mean—a very basic and clear value system that's more important than any role I might get or any award I might receive. I guess that makes me pretty proud.

DR. LESTER FISHER, RETIRED DIRECTOR OF THE LINCOLN PARK ZOO

Wild Kingdom

One Sunday morning in 1950, Marlin Perkins called me at home and told me I'd better get to the zoo right away. When I asked him why, he had just three words for me: "Bushman is out." I thought for a moment and asked myself, "Why call me?"

Escapes are a perpetual factor in zoo operations, due to human nature, not animal nature as one might suppose. No matter how safe and foolproof we try to make things, people, at times, show their humanity by making mistakes. During my tenure here, I became one of the few people in the world who has had the experience of seeing three major male gorillas out of their cages—at different times, in different decades, I'm happy to report.

Bushman started our gorilla dynasty back in 1931, arriving as a 38-pound 2-year-old. Before too long, though, he had grown to his potential—550 pounds and six feet tall. Needless to say, even seeing Bushman safely on the other side of the bars was enough to instill a healthy respect for his presence; seeing him without any barrier at all could provoke terror. It wasn't widely known, however, that there was something that could likewise provoke terror in him. That something was snakes. Years before, a zookeeper learned that Bushman was genuinely afraid of snakes, so when he got out, with an admirable presence of mind, the keeper dashed over to the Reptile House, got a handful of the non-poisonous variety and coaxed Bushman back to his home, to his security. By the time I arrived that Sunday morning, things had quieted down considerably.

The second great ape to escape was Sinbad, who just walked out of his cage and into the feed room of the old monkey house. By then, we had tranquilizer guns, so without too much trouble, we were able to shoot Sinbad with a dart, which put him to sleep and allowed us time to return him to his cages.

The last gorilla I was lucky enough to see out of his cage was the first one made famous by television. I was in my office, when the keeper called and told me, "There's a gorilla out and I think it's Sinbad." There are certain words that, as a zoo director, you don't like to hear. But I knew that Sinbad was getting old and had a little bit of arthritis, so I thought maybe I could outrun him. I took off towards the monkey house, and was rounding a corner near the Lion House, when I saw him coming toward me—not weak, aging Sinbad, but energetic, young (and famous) Otto. I did a double-take, stopped in my tracks and said, "Damn."

We were able to contain him within a relatively small area, between the Reptile House and the Lion House. The veterinarians were on the grounds and not far away. In the meantime, I tried to keep Otto's attention so he wouldn't venture any further. When the vets arrived they quickly darted him, but the tranquilizer didn't take immediate effect. Otto ran up an incline and ended up precariously perched on a raised ramp. As the drug started to take effect, Otto started leaning one way, and then the other, then forward, then back. By then, the police were all over the place with their weapons drawn, and I was yelling, "Please, don't shoot!" Thankfully, Otto, all 358 pounds of him, fell backward, unharmed, into some bushes, and we picked him up and carried him back.

Those were some of the most dramatic escapes. I'm proud to say that, today, the Lincoln Park Zoo probably has the best collection of gorillas in the country, and, on most days, all of them are safely in their homes, where visitors might expect them to be.

"We got the bill over to the House as quickly as possible only to find its opponents singing the famous 'Hey, Hey, Good-bye' song out on the floor."

JIM THOMPSON

JIM THOMPSON, LAWYER, FOUR-TERM ILLINOIS GOVERNOR

37

Central Sox Time

The planning and building of the new Comiskey Park is an archetypal Chicago story because it illustrates Chicago's motto, *I Will.* It is an example of the point at which city and state politics intersect—some would say collide—with a substantial, positive result in this case.

First of all, the idea of a new Comiskey Park forced the recognition of the necessity of razing the old Comiskey Park, a structure that had served the White Sox well since 1910 and was part of Chicago's history, skyline, and, really, its culture. But if you looked at it plainly, devoid of sentiment, the fact was that, although you could argue forever whether the old Park was structurally sound or whether it could be rehabilitated, it had outlived its financial usefulness. In order to keep the White Sox in Chicago, we had to build a new stadium, that was clear. The questions were where and how.

The "where" was the first question to be resolved: by moving the stadium right across 35th Street, the Sox maintained their essential history, character, and connection to the South Side. The "how" was the more difficult question, because, initially, the only people who really cared about keeping the White Sox here were the people with a specific interest in the team: the owners, some of the fans, and the City of Chicago. But the City didn't have the dollars or the will, so we had to turn to the State Legislature. Unfortunately, the majority of the members of the Legislature had no real interest because the Sox weren't their team. Even if they were from Chicago, those born north of Madison Street were Cub fans. If they were from the suburbs, they just didn't care enough to make the Sox a priority. And if they were downstaters, they absolutely didn't care because they were Cardinal fans.

It got down to the last possible day to pass the bill, and I was convinced it was dead. I was walking out of the Capitol to go home when I ran into some of the guys I had put in charge of this project, guys who believed in it like I did. Tom Reynolds, the chairman of the Sports Facilities Authority; and Tim Romani and Peter Bynoe, who were in charge of building the potential stadium, had really worked hard for this bill, and as I told them it was dead, I think all of us were struck simultaneously with the reality of what that would mean: the legacy of Comiskey Park would be lost and the White Sox would soon move to a near-tropical climate. The more we talked, the angrier we got, because this wasn't the way that politics was supposed to work. If something was right, then there should be a way to get it done. We looked at each other and nodded. We had eight hours.

I went back upstairs to see Pate Phillip, the Senate Republican Leader. I said, "Pate, I don't care if you're not a White Sox fan, I don't care if you live in DuPage, I don't care if you don't care what happens to the City of Chicago, I don't care if you have other priorities in this legislative session. This is wrong. They can't steal our team and take them to Florida. We can't let 'em, I'm not gonna let 'em, and you are going to help me not let 'em." He just looked at me and said, "All right, I'll help you." We started calling in senators one by one, and stated our position as clearly as possible, "Senator, this is important and we have to do this…we *must* do this. We wouldn't let another state steal a factory, we wouldn't let them steal the Art Institute, we wouldn't let them steal one of our cultural crown jewels, and we can't let them steal the Sox, part of Chicago's very fabric. You must vote for this bill so the Sox can remain where they belong." There wasn't anything in it for these guys—no trades and no deals. But by sheer force of will, which sometimes works in politics, we passed the bill in the Senate, by the skin of our teeth, at 20 minutes to midnight.

We got the bill over to the House as quickly as possible only to find its opponents singing the famous "Hey, Hey, Good-bye" song out on the floor. It wasn't a very optimistic atmosphere. As we walked onto the floor, we were serenaded with, "Na, na, na, na. Na, na, na, na; hey, hey, hey, gooo-ood bye." To add to an already dramatic situation, the Florida television stations were carrying live coverage from the House floor. The Tampa/St. Pete fans were absolutely sure that the bill wasn't going to pass and that the White Sox would soon be heading their way.

As the minutes ticked along, the situation became even more critical. I had been warned that it was going to be even tougher here in the House, and if the vote went beyond midnight the bill would have to win a three-fifths majority rather than a simple majority. The Speaker, Michael Madigan, was out of his chair working the Democratic side of the aisle and I was busy working the Republican side. We had an equitable arrangement: If he got a Democrat from downstate to switch I'd assuredly get a Republican from the same area to switch, so there wouldn't be any political problems back home. We continued our furious lobbying efforts as the inevitable deadline approached.

There are those who swear that it was beyond midnight when the actual vote was taken, but Representative McPike, who was temporarily occupying the Speaker's chair, and in charge of the proceedings, said that he was keeping time by his "reliable" watch, and that it was about ten seconds until midnight when the final vote was taken; a claim that caused the television viewers in Florida great distress. When the votes were counted it was clear that we had passed the bill by the narrowest of margins. The White Sox would remain the *Chicago* White Sox, after all.

I was honored to throw out the first pitch at the first game in the new ballpark. At ten-thirty that morning I got out there and practiced. Of course, it didn't do me any good. When my moment on the mound arrived, I threw low and outside. I took my seat and watched the White Sox pitcher get absolutely bombarded and thought to myself, you know, I couldn't have done any worse than this poor guy.

Today, I have season tickets, which I use as often as possible. Sometimes I find myself looking around this great new stadium and it strikes me how close it came to not existing. You really wouldn't think it would take three years and a bended-knee effort on the floor of the Senate and the House at the last possible minute to do something so simple, and so right, for the City of Chicago.

BOB LOVE, FORMER CHICAGO BULLS ALL-STAR

38

Gate 3-¹/₂

Everybody knows about *The Gate*. Nobody would care about it if it was only called "Gate Three," or "Gate Four." The mystique only works because it's an entrance named like no other: Gate 3-¹/₂. Chicago Stadium is a place with a lot of history; you can bet that those who made that history made their way into the place at the building's special gate, and each of them touched the doorknob on their way in.

I don't even know how Gate 3-¹/₂ originally got its name, but I know how it could affect me. Some days, I drove to the Stadium convinced I was going to have an average game, but when I got close to that dark door, surrounded by fans eager to catch a glimpse of  the players, my adrenaline started to flow. That energy and excitement changed me as I walked through. I became a raging Bull, ready to play. I made a habit of bringing some of the kids in with me so they could see the game. They didn't have tickets, but in those days they could find open seats, and even sit together. Isiah Thomas, Doc Rivers, Terry Cummings, Eddie Johnson, all significant players in the NBA today, but they were once part of that group of young kids that used to wait for me outside of Gate 3-¹/₂. I wasn't much of a talker so I couldn't express it in words, but the kids could feel the love I had for them in my heart. I was so proud to let them see myself, Norm Van Lier, Jerry Sloan, Chet Walker, and the game's greatest passing center, Tom Boerwinkle, out there on the floor—five of the best to ever play the game as a unit, as a team. We didn't win any championships but we were always in the game. If we stayed close until the fourth quarter, we would always win.

I'm still connected to the kids in this neighborhood. They still hang out, even the really young ones, waiting in the same spot. When they see me, they say, "Bob Love, man, there's Bob Love." And I still try, as often as I can, to get them inside. I put tickets in their hands, because, these days, they won't find any empty seats.

It's sad to have seen the Stadium outgrown. No matter how nice and new that building is across the street, it can't inherit the memories of this old place. Or can it?

And what happens to *The Gate*? I just don't know if the mystique can be moved a half a block south. But I hope it can.

Give Peace a Chance

Why is the nation's Peace Museum in Chicago? Why not Washington D.C. or New York—or Peoria, for that matter? There are logical reasons. Under the stands at University of Chicago's Stagg Field, the first fission tests were conducted as part of the Manhattan Project during World War II, tests which ushered in the Nuclear Age, brinksmanship, and the era of *necessary* peace. Also, during the 1968 Democratic National Convention and its aftermath, the nation focused its eyes on this city and the growing peace movement. And there are practical reasons as well. Chicago is a major, centralized city and it had a great group of folks ready to work hard and pull it off. I conceived the idea in 1974 and presented it to co-founder Marjorie C. Benton in 1979. After years of research, planning and fund-raising, The Peace Museum opened its doors on November 15, 1981.

Our first major show presented a series of drawings from survivors of Hiroshima, called *The Unforgettable Fire*. It was extraordinary for us to be able to exhibit these powerful works, none of which had ever been seen outside of Japan. The show's title has endured due in large part, to some wonderful allies of The Peace Museum—the Irish band, *U2*—which subsequently used the name for a book and an album. Their support has been more than casual; they brought several of our exhibitions to Dublin, initiating a traveling exhibition program at The Peace Museum. Now, in a typical year, while 20,000 will see our shows here in Chicago, 200,000 will see them around the country and around the world.

One of our most dramatic and widely-seen exhibitions was one in which we collaborated with Yoko Ono called "Give Peace a Chance." It started with a very simple idea that related to John Lennon's peace songs and campaigns, and once we got us in touch with Yoko Ono, the idea greatly expanded. Seven days after our proposal was mailed to New York, we received a call from The Dakota saying that Yoko was very excited about this project and wanted to help. Our concept of the exhibit was soon transformed into a tangible, three-dimensional show by including elements like the Gibson guitar that John used to write "Give Peace a Chance" and the original manuscripts of some of his most famous songs. We were ultimately able to present, in very dramatic fashion, some insight into the way John Lennon understood the idea of peace, and a glimpse at the way in which he

organized his campaigns. The show also included material from Arlo and Woodie Guthrie, Pete Seeger, and *U2*. There were audio-visual presentations and a wide range of memorabilia—more than 500 items in all.

The first day of the show, a Sunday, we were scheduled to open at one o'clock in the afternoon. People started lining up early that morning, and by the time we were set to open the doors, there was an excited crowd of more than 3,000 in the street. It was really quite amazing. The following day, Monday, like most museums, we were closed. I happened to be there with a security guard who had been hired to protect the tremendously valuable elements in the exhibit, when we heard a loud and constant pounding on the door. The guard went over and, speaking through the door, said rather gruffly, "Read the sign. We're open Tuesday through Sunday." The pounding didn't stop. This time, the guard made his point even clearer. Still, the pounding continued. I thought to myself, after all, this is a *peace* museum, so I went to the door, opened it and found three women standing there. Very gently, I told them to please come back the next day, when we would be open with the lights and sound system on. They then each reached into their coats and pulled out 24-hour round-trip tickets as proof, "We've just flown in from Dublin," one said, "and we're not leaving until we see John's guitar." My jaw dropped. All I could do was tell them to follow me. I led them through every phase of the show. When they came to the Lennon guitar, they laid flowers at its base, cried for about half an hour, and then let me escort them out. It sent shivers through the staff the next day when I told the story. And so launched *Give Peace a Chance*.

I think this particular exhibit demonstrated a public emotion. In the end, we had over 30,000 visitors come to see a show that 250 volunteers had helped produce. It had been a beautiful thing to behold: artists, architects, electricians, carpenters, painters and poets, all campaigning for peace and justice.

There has been a rich and difficult history locked into the never-ending battle for peace. In the post-Cold War era, the world is discovering that the struggle is necessarily an enduring one. I'm proud to say that The Peace Museum is continuing its mission.

"I had been in Chicago four months. It was the first day of 1967. Mike Royko and I were drinking blackberry brandy under the El tracks in a shot-and-beer joint, and the Blackhawks were on the radio."

ROGER EBERT

ROGER EBERT, FILM CRITIC

40

Making It

In late August of 1966, I loaded up the old Dodge with my clothes, my books, and my 1933 L.C. Smith typewriter, and headed up Route 45 to Chicago, making a promise to myself that within six months I would somehow get myself into one of those parties at the Playboy Mansion.

In the late spring, I was accepted by the University of Chicago as a Ph.D. candidate in English, and a few days later, a letter arrived at my Urbana address from Jim Hoge, then the city editor at the *Chicago Sun-Times*, asking me to come and see him about a job if I happened to be in Chicago.

I made the preliminary trip in July, taking the Illinois Central right into the old 12th Street Station. I walked up Michigan Avenue towards the river, then cut across to Wabash. At Lake Street, I could see the vast yellow letters in the sky announcing the *Chicago Sun-Times* and the *Chicago Daily News*. I paused underneath the El tracks and as the cars screeched overhead I felt filled with excitement. This was the Big City: skyscrapers and elevated trains and newsstands and cigar stores and race tracks—and the *Sun-Times*.

Over lunch at *Riccardo's*, I was offered a job, as a part-time feature writer. I was to start in September, under Dick Takeuchi, editor of the paper's Sunday supplement. I walked out giddy with pleasure. There was so much glory for me in being able to think of myself as a reporter for the *Sun-Times*, paper of Bill Mauldin and Kup and other heroes less well-known. The *Sun-Times* in those days was the hottest paper in Chicago, the "Bright One." The *Tribune* was still mired in the reactionary past of Colonel McCormick—who was gone, but not forgotten and certainly not superceded.

Right after Labor Day, I pointed the old Dodge north, found an apartment on 72nd Place in South Shore, started classes at the U of C, and went to the paper everyday. Dick Takeuchi had a weird array of assignments for me. I wrote about bottled water, snake handlers, comic book collectors, hero priests and Florence Scala, the heroine of Little Italy, who gave me coffee in her kitchen and tried to explain why Mayor Daley should not tear down her neighborhood to build Circle Campus. At some point I believe it occurred to her that she was talking to a kid who had arrived from Urbana three weeks earlier and hardly knew what a city neighborhood was, much less why it should be preserved. After she took me for a walking tour of the Hull House area, I wrote a story so breathless it read as if I had personally discovered the neighborhood, previously unknown.

I was drinking in those days. It was part of being a newspaperman, and part of being a student. As a student I drank at *Jimmy's*, the Hyde Park tap where the bartender was said to have a Ph.D. in philosophy. As a newspaperman, I drank at *Riccardo's* and *Billy Goat's*. It was helpful to drink because I was younger than almost everyone else on the paper, and keenly aware of being a small-town kid who was over his head in Chicago. Guys like Bob Zonka, a desk assistant, and John McHugh, who worked at the *Daily News*, became my pals. We laughed and bullshitted and made great manifestos and glorified the characters who were around in those days—characters like Jay Robert Nash, the crime expert, who looked and talked like Jimmy Cagney and was always pulling you aside for a few quiet confidences about the present whereabouts of Martin Bormann.

Meanwhile, in Hyde Park, I did all right in all of the classes except French. That took time. Everything else was fun. I never did finish my doctorate, mainly because, soon enough, I took the plunge into full-time newspapering and film criticism and all the rest of it. I've always felt that I left something incomplete behind me at the University. I would like to go back now, today, and sit down in the same classrooms and talk about the same things, picking up where I left off.

But the *Sun-Times* was taking more of my time, and attention, and paying my bills. And it was seducing me with its journalistic freemasonry. I was a reporter. I had a byline. The bartender at *Ric's* called me "Ebert." John Fischetti, the cartoonist for the *Daily News*, would make room for me in his booth on Friday afternoons, which was when reporters from all four newspapers would jam into *Riccardo's* to drink and talk. I met Studs Terkel and Nelson Algren. They sat down like ordinary people and talked to anyone who could keep up their conversational speed. There were girls. And there was the excitement of the late 1960s themselves, which was genuine, and which, even at the time, I believe we knew was unique. I was one of "the kids" at a time when a youth revolution seemed to be sweeping across the country. I was there.

I remember being at work late on the first day of 1967 with a heavy snow falling. There weren't many people there. Over on the *Daily News* side of the floor, there were only two or three, because the *Daily News* wouldn't be publishing the next day. One of them was Mike Royko. I knew him slightly from *Ric's*. Of course, everybody knew him from his column, which he had just started writing a few years earlier, and which felt new and anarchic, cynical and very funny. Everybody who worked for the Chicago papers in those days knew Royko was the best. He had come out of the neighborhoods and the City News Bureau; he was the real thing.

He asked me what I was doing. I said I'd just finished a story. He said he had to pick up a prescription for his wife at the pharmacy in the old neighborhood. Did I want to come along? Maybe we'd get a pop along the way.

I did. He dropped off the prescription at the drugstore at North and Milwaukee, and we went into a bar under the El tracks—a bar so small the owner could service all the customers without getting up from his stool. Royko told me it was an eye-opener joint, where workingmen would stop for a bracer before getting on the bus or the El in the morning. We were both hung over, and he said blackberry brandy was good for that. He was right.

The bartender was listening to a Blackhawks hockey game on the radio. Royko was telling me about the crooks and thieves at City Hall, and about the characters in the North and Milwaukee neighborhood, which was where he had grown up. I was filled suddenly with a transcendent happiness. I had been in Chicago four months. It was the first day of 1967. Mike Royko and I were drinking blackberry brandy under the El tracks in a shot-and-beer joint, and the Blackhawks were on the radio. Suddenly, all seemed complete, transparent, achievable, real.

With half of my mind I was keeping track of the game, even though I had never been to a professional hockey game (or a professional baseball or basketball or football game).

"Jesus Christ," I said. "That game is wide open. They're scoring a goal every 15 seconds!"

"You dumb shit," the bartender said. "This is the replay of the game highlights."

Royko laughed and laughed. So did I. So did the bartender. I didn't know what the fuck I was doing in Chicago, drinking in a joint under the El, pretending to understand hockey, but I knew that I was in the right place at the right time. And ever since, when the elevated trains roar past overhead, I feel a shadow of the same feeling, still there.

MARVA COLLINS, EDUCATOR

Rays of Light

Over the years, this unassuming school building tucked away on West Chicago Avenue has become an oasis in a desert of despair and negativity. Its edifice is not as impressive as some you might find in other areas around town, but I find it interesting that it's a place that so many people want to visit. This school has been host to a wide range of politicians, including American Presidents, various officials and foreign dignitaries, and a great number of those interested in the substantive education of our young people. But why has this school become such a place of wonder and interest? Aren't we just doing here what each and every school should be doing? Yes, but here, we steadfastly maintain that any child can learn if they are not taught too thoroughly that they cannot. Here, we absolutely refuse to accept anything short of excellence. And here, we offer each child the promise: *We will not allow you to fail.*

In 1975, I decided that enough was too much and I took my last $5,000 in savings from my teachers' pension fund and began a school on the second floor of my home. I took my own two children out of prestigious Chicago private schools, and along with 18 other neighborhood children, Westside Preparatory School was born. After 14 years as a Chicago public school teacher, I had seen far too many children destined for failure, far too many children with eyes devoid of hope. All around me the doomsday cries said, "these children cannot learn," and I simply could not believe this to be true.

Within two years, Westside Preparatory School was featured on *60 Minutes, Good Morning America*, and every major network. In addition, the school was featured in *Time, Forbes, The Wall Street Journal, The New York Times*, and newspapers from around the country and around the world. In other words, what should have been the norm all over America was considered a "miracle." Because most children in the "dying inner-cities" see themselves as failures, most have lived out that expectation. But we have consistently proved that that needn't be the case; the children here learn very early when they read Plato's *Republic* that education is of primary importance. And each of the children will tell you that the process of education begins with literacy.

Recently, I have turned my attention to training teachers, principals and administrators from all over the world. And we continue to have thousands of visitors each year who come to Westside Preparatory to see that, yes, even these city kids from Chicago's toughest neighborhoods can provide rays of light, rays of excellence. I believe that we can change the world one child at a time, and that failure and mediocrity can only persist when good people do nothing. Further, I believe that if we have not lit the candle of excellence in America, we have no right to curse the darkness.

I have been able to touch the lives of millions of children through the training of their teachers, principals and administrators, and though these are not children whom I gave "birth" to, these are children whom I have allowed to grow in my heart. I know that my future is inextricably bound to these children—America's future is inextricably bound to these children.

We each, I believe, have a reason for being on this earth; I know that my reason is to fight for the education of our young with every sinew in my body and soul.

"The cop's hand moved to the lapel of his new second-hand overcoat. The official fingers rubbed appreciatively. 'Gettin' a little big for five, buddy,' said our Chicago Guardian. Higgins doubled the offering and was absolved. 'Ah, Chicago'"

RICHARD STERN

My Chicago

Chicago? That was where Great-Uncle Herman fled from hawk-faced Aunt Milly to be fetched back to his connubial jail by Grandma. I loved Herman. (Who else cackled over egg bins at the grocer's, or sucked them through pinholes he made in the shell? Who else let me win a figure ring from whose belly I would—years later—remove a diamond for my fiancée?) So early, I had the sense of Chicago as a refuge from New York troubles.

Age six, parents away for a rare week, I was left with Ida—who whacked me with metal corset stays—and Mary, my usual caretaker. Ida, pointing to a front page picture, told me to tell Mary, "Your boyfriend's been shot in Chicago." (The "boyfriend" was John Dillinger.) So menace was part of that strange greatness on the distant lake.

Chicago was also where Colonel McCormick came from, he of the highfalutin' accent which editorialized among Strauss waltzes on one of my favorite radio programs.

Was I in seventh or eighth grade when *Life* featured a page of solemn men in black robes under the headline "Is the University of Chicago the World's Greatest?" To one who knew only Columbia, NYU and Harvard and eventually ended at Chapel Hill, this was a bolt from a different blue. *What was going on out there* in the city of pig squeals and gangsters?

Chicago fact and fiction accumulated before I actually set eyes on the place. I'd seen Chapel Hill and Bangor, Maine, had worked in a department store in Evansville, Indiana, a radio station in Orlando, Florida, then, after a year in Cambridge, Massachusetts, had gone to Versailles as a Fulbright Fellow. After that, I worked in Heidelberg and Frankfurt, married, become a father, seen Brussels, Belgrade, Beirut and Berlin—but not Chicago. Then, back in the U.S., en route to Iowa City, I changed trains there. I walked out of the old La Salle Street Station, up State Street and down Wabash. I saw the Palmer House, the El, the broken faces of failure, the striding shine of success, felt the speed, thrust, racket and power of a terrific city, not New York, not Paris, something else, I didn't know what.

Eighteen months later, I drove up with other graduate students for the Modern Language Association Convention. We were looking for jobs. I stayed with my pal, Tom Higgins, a pianist, then paying his bills as a bellhop at the Hotel Del Prado. He told me that he'd just been stopped on Lake Shore Drive by a cop. Knowing the city, Higgins held out his wallet, a five dollar bill coupled to his driver's license. The cop's hand moved to the lapel of his new second-hand overcoat. The official fingers rubbed appreciatively. "Gettin' a little big for five, buddy," said our Chicago guardian. Higgins doubled the offering and was absolved. "Ah, Chicago," chortled I.

After ten humiliating interviews persuaded me I was an unhireable zero, I retreated to the Art Institute and stood before *Sunday Afternoon on the Grand Jatte* as suspended in fixative color as the butterflies, walkers, dogs, boats and smokers of that great canvas. Chicago had such consolations.

In an elevator, I asked a lady with a badge for an interview. "Send me your life," said she. (The word she used was *vita*.) I was hired for a year in New London, Connecticut. The next spring, my old pal Don Justice wrote that he'd just turned down the year's best academic job at the University of Chicago. "The city intimidates us," he wrote. "So does the University." Three days later, I got a telegram asking me to come for interviews. I borrowed the fare and met the men—no women then—who were to be my friends and colleagues. That day, my chief sponsor, Norman Maclean, drove me into the city, telling me how it was both entwined and removed from the University. Too insensitive to be intimidated, I was wowed by everything. (In addition, they would pay me $4,800, $1,300 more than I was making.)

In August, I drove my newly-purchased fourth-hand Chevy past the blazing mills of Gary and the dumb white Standard Oil vats of Whiting to South Chicago. In front of the South Shore Country Club, cops stopped cars till a huge Cadillac, license plate Number 1, eased out of the gate. "Who's that?" asked I. "His Eminence," said the cop. "The Cardinal." I advanced a grade. So this too was Chicago.

And now I was as well. 1955. Mayor Daley the First was, like me, just beginning. He prospered, grew great; I hung on, held on. I taught classes, wrote books, raised children, made friends, moved every few years, always within 20 minutes' walk of my office. I met, watched and listened to some of the world's most interesting and talented people. (Some were colleagues, students, neighbors, friends.) I knew a bit of joy, grief, excitement, fatigue, intrigue, nobility, treachery, triumph, defeat. Much life, too much death.

Love.

Long ago, back when I played cards with Uncle Herman, I held up a spoonful of my favorite dessert and announced, "I love Brown Betty." Said my father, "You mean you *like* Brown Betty. You can't love what can't love you."

But I did love Brown Betty, and, despite burglaries, break-ins, stolen cars, broken bones, disappointment, bewilderment, fear and rage, I not only love Chicago, I feel that I am somehow a loved part of it, an old fixture, like a wind-shaken but still standing locust tree or a replastered, repainted, rewired, retubed three-flat that stands amid a slum clearance or a gentrification. Uncle Herman's temporary refuge has become my permanent one. By God, Chicago, I do love you, I do.

Power of the Music

It was the power of the music that helped me keep my feet on the ground during my turbulent teens, and it was at 950 West Wrightwood where I got my regular helpings of live rock 'n' roll nourishment at a place called *Alice's Revisited*. *Alice's* was a haven for hippie activities, a hangout where you could get a sandwich, drink some coffee—no alcohol was served—and read Chicago's underground rag, *The Seed*, which was published in an office upstairs. For me, though, *Alice's* was where I went to get lost in the music. It's where I went to escape the pain of an embattled home life, where I could go and not have to keep up my school day countenance as class clown. At *Alice's* I would close my eyes and flail about the room with abandon, my long hair whirling as a blur, dancing by myself to bands like *Body*, *Rawl Hardman*, and Harvey Mandel's *Pure Food and Drug Act* with Sugarcane Harris on electric violin.

My first big time rock concert was at the *Aragon* to see Leslie West's *Mountain* (West, the 300 pound guitarist, actually was a mountain), and I'd seen the newly renamed *Chicago* at DePaul's *Alumni Hall*. Still, these shows couldn't match the intensity of seeing a group like *Mountain Bus* doing a long, *Grateful Dead*-like set in the packed back room at *Alice's*. There I studied the musicians' pained expressions and imagined, as I trained my eye on the lead guitarist's dexterous fingers, that I could play as well simply by watching. I still do that today.

Other greats I remember seeing at *Alice's* were *Siegal-Schwall Blues Band*, *Wilderness Road*, and *Tiny Alice* from Cleveland. One night in the summer of '72 really stands out. I had recently been blown away by a hot tune I'd heard on WGLD featuring an explosive lead guitar solo by one John Curulewski of a South Side band with a newly-released debut album on *Wooden Nickel* records. Much to my delight, they were to appear at *Alice's*. I got my buddy, Lou Benson, to join me. I promised him he'd love this new band called *Styx* and true to form, that night Curulewski was a monster. Never have I spent a better two dollars. Unfortunately, John Curulewski left the band soon thereafter, or maybe was fired. Either way, we all know what happened to *Styx* in the years following that appearance at *Alice's* in 1972. It was all downhill from there.

JOHN H. JOHNSON, PUBLISHER, FOUNDER OF EBONY AND JET MAGAZINES

Lessons in Success

When I was growing up in the Deep South, the days of lynchings had not yet ended. There existed a lingering fear within the black community, and that is among the reasons why Chicago was viewed by blacks with the same kind of wonder that Ellis Island was viewed by Europeans: it was a place of magic, a gateway to authentic opportunity. When I finally arrived here in July of 1933, at age 15, I reveled in the success among black people that I saw: doctors, lawyers, school teachers, and business people. To go from a place of segregation and denial of opportunity, to one of relative freedom and vast potential, was truly inspiring.

What strikes me, upon re-examining that crucial time in my life, is the astounding dedication I found among teachers when I first came here. These days, I hear nothing but bad news about public schools, whether in this city or elsewhere. I think that we, as a society have somehow, somewhere along the way, lost respect for teachers, and teachers, in turn, may have lost a little bit of respect for students. If teachers have to constantly fight to get an increase in wages, if they have to constantly fight to get respect for themselves, then perhaps it is asking too much of them to inspire and motivate students.

In the days that I attended DuSable High School—which is in the heart of the ghetto, then and now—the teachers were respected, and therefore, they were dedicated. They gave us pride in ourselves and they made us believe that we could overcome any handicaps that we might confront. It never occurred to me that DuSable wasn't as good a school as any of the other schools in the city, or that I could not do what any other student in the city could do.

I remember one teacher, in particular, and it seems that all the students who went through that school, including the late Mayor Harold Washington, Dempsey Travis, Redd Foxx and Nat Cole, remembered her as well: her name was Mary J. Herrick, and she taught civics. She was white, but we never thought of her as anything other than "Miss Herrick," somebody dedicated and devoted to education and to the students she taught. She didn't just teach civics by the book, she taught civics about life. She told us about blacks who had been important in American history. She took us on field trips downtown. She was perhaps the first white person to ever invite me to their home on a social basis. She was just a woman who believed in people. And because she believed in us, we believed in ourselves. Miss Herrick could be stern, and, at times, a real disciplinarian. But she balanced that toughness with what can only be described as love, and, in doing so, opened up a whole new world for her students, many of whom were, like myself, from a place far, far from Chicago.

When I was a high school senior, Miss Herrick helped me make an important first step toward becoming an adult. I had just won a tuition scholarship to the University of Chicago and she called me into her classroom to discuss what she knew was an important outward sign of personal identity: my name. I had been Johnny Johnson for 17 years and understood myself as Johnny Johnson. She said to me, "Johnny, you're practically grown up now, you're going off to college—shouldn't you be 'John?'" I said that John sounded good to me. She continued, "Perhaps you should have a middle name. How about 'Henry?'" "No, I don't like 'Henry'...but maybe 'Harold.'" So from that day forward, I was John Harold Johnson. Since they didn't keep birth records in Arkansas when I was born, I applied for my first birth certificate with my mother and several of her friends swearing to my birth date, while Miss Herrick presided over the "birth."

The enthusiasm and attention shown by Miss Herrick had practical business applications I realized only years later. Johnson Publishing has been in business for more than 50 years now, but when we first started, this company was one of very few that offered authentic opportunities for blacks interested in journalism, marketing and business. In the 1960s, when the Civil Rights laws started to come into effect, there were many companies out there that tried everything they could to hire away our highly trained employees, and, initially, they had some success.

As this started to happen, I remembered back to Miss Herrick and how she had influenced her students by showing how deeply she cared for them. I made a list of the 30 most important people that I needed to run this company, and I put their names up on an easel in my office. Each day when I came into work, inspired by Miss Herrick's philosophy, I would ask myself what I could do to let these people know that I cared about them, let them know that their problems were my problems, that their ambitions were my ambitions.

In the process, for the first time I got to know these people—really know them—who was married, who had kids, and what kinds of personal ambitions each possessed. Because of my genuine interest in, and connection to, these individuals, I didn't lose one of the employees on that list. Except for those who died, they are all here now.

I know in my heart that I learned some of that attention and caring and believing from Miss Herrick, and I know her lessons have served me well.

45

The Naked City

I first saw Chicago at two on a June morning in 1966. I was coming from a small town in eastern Kansas to do summer service work for the Presbytery of Chicago—volunteer work in a time of great hope, great excitement, a time when we thought change possible, when we believed that if we poured enough energy, and enough good will, into the terrible problems of our country, we could change those problems for good.

The vastness of the city at night was overwhelming. Red flares against a yellow sky, and mile on mile of unbending lights: street lamps, neon signs, traffic lights, flashing police blues —lights that didn't illuminate, but threw shadows, and made the city seem a monster, ready to devour the unwary.

In the small town of my youth, privacy was impossible: everyone's business, in sickness and in health, was the business of the whole community. In some ways this was good: When my brother was rude to a teacher he encountered downtown one Saturday afternoon, my mother heard about it from three separate sources within the hour. Ill manners never recurred.

In other ways, neighborly involvement was a polite name for nosy. When I was 20, every-one in town knew I had started dating a young biology instructor. The attention so incensed him that he stopped seeing me.

Coming from a small town, I found Chicago's vastness, its lights and sounds, both terri-fying and exhilarating: they offered the promise of a personal privacy I had never known. It was only after some months, when I grew used to the frenzy of a city that never sleeps, that I realized anonymity also brings with it great loneliness.

 In the winter, I used to watch for a man sleeping on a bench beneath a drawbridge, on Lake Shore Drive's old S curve, before those towers were demolished. Where is he now? Did he freeze to death? Did anybody know his name? The ominous extension of privacy is oblivion.

In my early days here, as I tried to pick my way through the vast sprawl to a community of my own, I became friends with Barbara Wasserman, a young artist who knew the city far better than I. Barbara introduced me to the Sunset Baths on the city's northwest side.

These baths played an important role in the social life of the neighborhood's eastern

SARA PARETSKY, WRITER

European Jews. Like the public baths of Russia they provided an inexpensive social outing for the community. At Sunset, you could use a sauna and steam room as well as a swimming pool—and, of course, showers and outsize bathtubs. People played cards or drank fizzy water as they had in Russia, but it's doubtful the baths of Odessa ever included a bowling alley.

Tuesday was ladies night at the Sunset Baths—the rest of the week the place belonged to men. On Tuesdays, women could leave behind a dreary round of jobs—cleaning office buildings or giving pedicures—for a night of freedom and friendship. A modest fee gave admission to all facilities; for another five dollars you got a first-class massage.

Women came with their daughters and grand-daughters. They met old friends, they played cards, drank seltzer with raspberry syrup, sat in the sauna to sweat off the grime of the week. One woman always wore a startling blue mud mask, like woad, in the sauna.

Barbara and I felt timid in this company. We were outsiders. We spoke neither Russian nor Yiddish, and had no way of following, let alone taking part, in what seemed like ribald exchanges.

We were awed by the impassive dignity with which the older women carried their large, naked bodies. You had to strip to the skin in the baths. Those who played cards might wrap towels around themselves, but that was only as a protection against drafts.

Sunset women were not ashamed of their bodies, although they violated every canon of what we are brainwashed into thinking makes up the perfect female form. Their breasts sagged, their hips were massive, their bellies distended from many pregnancies. They held their massive bodies erect, with self-assured dignity.

I had absorbed from an early age the lessons of self-criticism, of dislike for every part of me that strayed from a mythical ideal of beauty. I especially hated my breasts, which sprouted large when all the models were flat-chested wraiths. From the time I'd started wearing a bra, I'd slouched like an ungainly chimpanzee, trying to conceal my chest.

One night, as I sweated in the sauna while Barbara swam, one of the women took my arm. "You are Jewish?" she said with a heavy accent.

When I nodded, yes, she went on, "Why you sit like that?"

She mimicked my hunched shoulders. "In my home, where I come from, Jews must be scared, but here in America, no. Here in America you stand up straight, be proud, look in the eye."

Then she resumed her conversation in Russian with her friend. Burning with embarrassment, I crept from the sauna and took refuge in the pool, swimming lap after lap until Barbara was ready to leave for the night.

We only went back one more time after that. We knew we didn't belong, that we had to find our community somewhere else in the city—in the clothed city.

The Sunset Baths have been closed for years now, but that woman remains with me. When I catch sight of myself in a store window, and see myself drooping, I think, "Here in America you stand up straight," and for a time I hold my shoulders back, and stride down the street with the assurance of a woman at home, in her body and her city.

Yin and Yang at Comiskey

I'm from the North Side, so I've always been more of a Cub fan than a White Sox fan. But I became more interested in the South Siders after I got involved with them through a fund-raising project for an arts organization—the Renaissance Society at the University of Chicago. I donated a painting of Harold Baines, the All-Star centerfielder, to the cause.

On September 30, 1990, I found myself at the last game at the old Comiskey Park, with my son Marc. It was a cold, windy day, so I had on a bulky coat, a hat, and some sunglasses. I remember it was a big deal, being the last game, very nostalgic for everyone. It was, of course, a sellout crowd and everyone had their cameras and camcorders. *Everything* was a souvenir, every piece of cement, every splinter of wood and every scrap of paper.

At this time of my life, I had a big retrospective of my paintings that was soon to open at the Art Institute of Chicago, and there had been quite a bit of media attention. People even recognized me here and there.

The game had not yet started and there were three vendors standing nearby, just talking. One of them kept looking over in my direction, and eventually, I looked at him. He raised his fist and yelled, "ED, ED! CONGRATULATIONS! The show opening at the Art Institute—that's good, man." I looked at him and thought, this is amazing. I'm wearing all this paraphernalia and this guy somehow recognizes me? Ballpark vendors are that conscious about art!?

I thought this was really a scary indication that the public's awareness of me had saturated itself to such extent. At the same time, my ego was dealing with this weird celebrity trip. And then, I felt something hit me on the head, and then on the shoulder. I looked up, and it was a pigeon in the rafters that had relieved himself on me. I thought, wait a minute… the yin and yang of ego. I immediately connected these two experiences, in an odd sort of a way, and understood them as the symbiotic forces of nature at work. I had been feeling so caught up in celebrity mode that, to me, it was a very clear symbolic thing. So I thanked the pigeon for cutting me down to size, or at least for providing a neutralizing and balancing component to this other, overarching ego. It all snapped into focus for me. As for my hat and coat, well, that's another story. In retrospect, who knows? Maybe it wasn't a higher force at all. Maybe it was the curse of the Cubs reminding me which part of town I'm from.

Rescued from the Dark Sea of Silence

I pulled the sheets up closer to my eyes and squinted over them. No child likes to lose the game of pretending to sleep when a parent enters the room. My father's back was turned to me and all I could see was the great wide belt on the back of his herringbone coat. He fumbled through my drawer, second from the top, in our wooden dresser, which our family of four shared, in our little corner flat in Albany Park. I looked above the sheets once more. The drawer closed. My father turned around and removed his grey hat, as he reached down to kiss my brow. I remember the crisp aroma of his face, his freshly shaved cheek against my forehead, as he kissed me from the side of his mouth. That was the last time I saw my father. I was 10 years old; my brother Joe was 16…

My brother and I shared a bed during those early years, my mother was in the bed next to us and my dad slept on a foldaway in the only other room. As luck would have it, my mother was a very light sleeper, who would wake at 5 a.m. to go to work each day. That meant no movement, no talking and no laughing in our bed—anytime she was in the room.

I remember when Joe turned 13, he paid me a dime to open the back door after curfew. I crawled on both hands and knees, to the back door, which I opened link by link at the appointed hour. It creaked open and suddenly a hand pushed my shoulder out the door which slammed behind me. My brother and I watched in defeat as she locked the door from the inside, securing each bolt and chain. A violent argument followed inside the house, and moments later, my father was tossed out, too. She was tough.

In the summer months, arguments and cries would erupt from up and down the alley. They poured from the open windows of emotionally charged households, into the streets. Our block was a ghetto for ill-matched husbands and wives who mostly married out of consolation, not love. When World War II ended, most met each other in refugee and displacement camps. The best years of their lives had been taken from them.

Our father was a merchant once; a small lumber exporter residing in an Eastern European port. He was an educated and religious man. When he lost everything in the War—his business, his parents, his friends and seemingly his life—he also changed. He too, had pulled the protective sheets closer to his eyes. Occasionally, he would surface to love us,

H. GENE & JOE SILVERBERG, CLOTHIERS

his boys. He didn't verbally express his love. We never spoke of sports or school; never played catch or went to a movie. Instead, he showed his love by gently holding me on his lap, quietly sitting for hours. I would look deeply into his sad grey eyes for great lengths of time and imagine him as the accomplished young man he once was. He might have been a trusted friend to someone, but who? No photos survived and no friends—only the reflection in his eyes. *"Grow up, grow up,"* I'd plead to myself, so I could rescue him from his dark sea of silence, lift the sheets and extract his inner sadness.

The morning my father left, after kissing me on the brow, I awoke and walked to school. It was about seven blocks to Haugan School on the corner of Wilson and Hamlin. I detested that bitter walk in the winter. The ice cracking at my feet, the punishing wind biting at my ears like a mad dog. I was taught not to complain. Didn't Dad have to work in the camp each day with only rags wrapped around his bare feet? Each day, he would lightly soak the rags with water to form an outer protective boot of ice. A boot of ice! Dare I believe that my feet were cold? When his rags were stolen one night and he refused to work in the frozen detail, he was placed in solitary confinement, where, some months before, his father had died. His stepmother and 12-year-old stepbrother had already died of exposure, and were it not for the existence of his younger brother, he might have given up. Instead, for two weeks, in a frozen cell, he managed to stay alive. He succeeded, but he was never the same.

At about eleven o'clock that night, we summoned the police. Our father had not returned home, and by daybreak on December 11, we realized that maybe he was gone forever.

My brother and I began searching for him that morning and continued well into the night. We searched the night after that, and then the next night, and the night after: in gangways and corridors, up and down the Albany Park streets, we searched. In alleys, in hallways, on corners, on stoops—we could not walk fast enough. No rest. The bus stop, the El stop, the basement of his synagogue, Jensen Park, Gompers Park, through every row in the Terminal Theater; all the storefronts whirled about us as though we were on a carousel out of control. Up Lawrence, down Kedzie, across Montrose—"Quick, check with the cops on Sunnyside and Pulaski." No word, no sign. What next?

I stood in front of the bar on Drake and Lawrence where he had been struck by a car only three weeks before. A small spot of his blood remained on the pavement below me.

His three day recovery, following that event, became an excuse for his boss to lay him off. Desperate, ashamed, he never told us. Instead, he ran. Suddenly, I remembered my dresser drawer! I ran to it and there I found $53 with a rubber band tightly holding the bills together. I bit my lip. It was Dad's last week's pay. Now the search must go downtown.

The following day, my brother and I rode the Ravenswood El to trace his routine steps exactly. We checked the cars, the platform—the stops along the way were all too familiar. I knew each roof, each window, each fire escape. These were our tracks. We rode them to Maxwell Street each and every weekend, bundled up to brave the long winter days in the outside market. There, among the greenhorn Jews, the Gypsies, the Poles, the Hispanics, the Italians and Blacks, we learned lessons about life and people that would last us a lifetime.

Holding each other up, we sorted through the lost and forgotten souls along skid row on West Madison Street. The fading light of the day made it hard to distinguish the men from the cardboard cartons with which they covered their cold bodies. We'd check the boxes and lift the newspapers from these poor lost men in search of a herringbone coat.

Soon, our mission became fearless. Our confidence grew and our sorrow became less of an impediment. We acquired a stronger will to live, and now, I realize how much that sense of determination has grown in us.

"Was that your plan, Pop? A legacy, to teach us strength by your absence? It was too high a price for all of us, Pop. It was more fun sleeping on the porch."

On the ninetieth day of the search, our father was found, drowned, on an ice-swept 47th Street beach. He had on his coat, his herringbone winter coat.

I did not cry. And, in the mixed emotions that rain down during a time like this, I felt a surge of relief. For him, the pain was over. For us, the search was over.

Nineteen years later, on exactly the same day my father disappeared, my wife gave birth to our first son. He is a great comfort to me today. His eyes are deep and thoughtful. Sad, in a familiar way. I recognize it and am comforted by it. He seems wise and gentle; old and young. He often lays comfortably across my chest. I look deeply into his eyes and sometimes see an image of a man holding another 10-year-old boy. I feel the tug of ages. I feel a sense of recovery. Rescued from the pain and the sleepless nights. Rescued from the search. Rescued from the past. Rescued at last from the dark sea of silence.

ARDIS KRAINIK, GENERAL DIRECTOR, LYRIC OPERA OF CHICAGO

Toward the 21st

Chicago is not simply the "first," "second," or "third" city in America; it is one of the 20 or 30 world-class international cities. What makes a city world-class is the inclusion of the great cultural institutions, opera being one of them.

I came to the Lyric Opera on May 26, 1954. So I was here from the start and in on all the fun. In 1946, the last pre-Lyric local opera company closed down, and for the next seven years, Chicago existed without a resident company. But with a great deal of determination, perseverance, and abundant powers of persuasion, Carol Fox and several others forged from the ground up, what was originally called the Lyric Theatre of America. And somehow Carol had persuaded the young, incendiary Maria Callas, who was just beginning to enjoy a worldwide reputation, to open the new company with performances of *Norma*. When I arrived, we were just starting to sell tickets for the fall performances, and though I knew nothing of Maria Callas, I was soon telling people how wonderful she was going to be.

I got my job not because I was a young singer of any musical ability, not because I had done graduate work in music at Northwestern University, and not because I had capably taught high school speech and drama. I got my job because I could type. And type I did for five blessed years, in addition to addressing and sealing envelopes, licking stamps and just about anything I could to help the fledgling Lyric Opera of Chicago. Money was so tight that the *real* typist in the office, one much more capable than I, warned me to cash my check the minute I got it. When I inquired why, she looked at me incredulously and reminded me that this was an opera company and opera companies were known to go out of business in a hurry. But it never occurred to me that this particular one would ever go under, and I continued my practice of cashing my paychecks as I needed them.

My mother was relieved to see me working for a woman as respectable as Carol Fox, someone with a solid Chicago family background. My mother specifically told Carol, "Now you just tell Ardis what to do." And Carol proceeded to do just that for the next 27 years. But I had a wonderful relationship with her. I was like her younger sister in many ways. She gradually brought me into the business and gave me many opportunities to learn. So many, in fact, that by 1980 I had worked my way up from being the Lyric's second-string typist to being its general director.

Over the years, we have been so artistically and economically successful here that I am happy to report it has astounded many of my American and European colleagues. Opera companies must be run like businesses, and each company must inevitably make compromises. But an opera company's artistic decisions, which, at some point, must acknowledge economic realities, are what tests its artistic integrity. In 1989, we faced perhaps the ultimate test to date of this integrity.

There is no question in my mind that Luciano Pavarotti made a great deal of difference to Lyric Opera and its success in the 1970s. He is clearly one of the most important operatic artists in the world, and for me to have had to discipline an artist of his stature was indeed a sad and painful thing. But, over the years, Luciano had cancelled 26 out of 41 Lyric performances for which he had signed contracts.

When Luciano cancelled the opening of our 35th anniversary season, I decided, with great regret, and together with the other decision-makers here, to break off negotiations. What this decision demonstrated was that the artistic integrity of the Lyric Opera was intact. The defection of one individual, no matter who that individual was, could not affect the condition of the whole. There isn't anyone who does business in Chicago who would put up with an employee who cancelled with such consistency. This is a very conservative city, in its own way, and we stand for plenty of old-fashioned values.

But that is not to say that we are "old-fashioned" in terms of what we produce on our stage! In 1989, we announced our "Toward the 21st Century" artistic initiative—an unprecedented decade-long commitment to 20th Century American and European opera, including the commissioning of three world premieres. I am delighted to say that the operas that have been produced as part of this program have proven to be "hits" with both our audiences and critics.

In addition, we are looking ahead to an exciting future as owners of the opera house and auxiliary space, which we have occupied as renters for nearly 40 years. We have initiated an ambitious capital campaign to finance the actual purchase and, in addition, provide funds for the extensive renovation of the backstage area. I'm proud to say that this will ensure our ability to provide world-class opera for a world-class city well into the next century.

"'What does Chicago think it is, anyway, San Francisco?' my friend Carmen, a Chicago poet who gains local respect as a unionized construction engineer, asked me recently. 'Cafes everywhere! It's disgusting.'"

ANA CASTILLO

ANA CASTILLO, POET AND WRITER

No Place for a Poet

My hometown is not poetry. That is not to say that Chicago is not poetic in its own Sandburgish way. It is definitely that place of which rich fiction á la Americana is made.

But no, my hometown is not poetry.

At least I did not think so the first 30 years of my poet's life. So, with pre-potty trained child in tow, I did the only thing a self-respecting, penniless, unknown and in my opinion (apparently the most popular opinion that poets have of themselves), unappreciated poet seeking ambience would do. I relocated to San Francisco.

Timing, I don't think, is one of those things that I will ever be remembered for having. Not that I did not find in that inimitable city by the Bay a cafe-insurgent-art-renegade-writer-type ambience. Long languid, liquid, luscious afternoons on end with nothing to do (when the baby was at daycare at least) but talk poetry with poets, savvy *politicos*, and a few who were just unemployed. "The City" (as it is referred to by Northern Californian residents… only tourists referred to it as "Frisco") embraced me like the prodigal daughter, one more poet to its multitudinous artistic family and welcomed me home. Ah—now *that* city truly is a poem—in free verse to a world beat meter. My five year stint as poet-in-training there, raising my little boy, cultivating an herb garden in flower pots on the perennially brisk terrace, paying the bills with substitute teaching, and producing two well-received books of poems, were well worth that long haul from the Midwest to the West Coast that Labor Day weekend years ago with everything but the kitchen sink along for the ride.

But a strange thing happened right after I moved to San Francisco. Chicago became *the* city for poets. Or at least that was the general drift blowing from the Windy City westward with stories of new small presses flourishing on the North and South Sides and of the quickly infamous "Poetry Slam" competitions. It was confirmed for me finally one day while I was on a flight out of San Francisco. I was perusing the latest copy of a Bay Area poetry rag when my eyes fell upon the following ad:

★ ★ ★ POETRY ★ ★ ★
COMPETITION
Win A Round-Trip
Ticket to Chicago
CALL (312) 235

To *Chicago*? I read on. Yes, of course, the new lifetime dream of any self-respecting San Francisco poet—the chance to compete in a Chicago-style poetry competition, on stage in a bar in the newly gentrified Near Northwest part of town where cafes (a notion unheard of before; the "espresso" was only served in places like Serbian neighborhood restaurants where you would also get your fortune told by the cook-owner, like it or not, in the grounds of your demitasse) were now multiplying like rabbits everywhere you turned.

"What does Chicago think it is, anyway, San Francisco?" my friend Carmen, a Chicago poet who gains local respect as a unionized construction engineer, asked me recently. "Cafes everywhere! It's disgusting." We were sitting in a formerly Greek-owned diner just before I was to enter next door what was once an abandoned warehouse turned art-happening-place that had actually *flown* me in to read.

I looked around. Abstract paintings on the wall by a local artist. A ton of art and literary rags on the floor near the door. Flyers on the windows announcing experimental theater and performance art events. "Hmm," I said, "I used to dream of this years ago, before I left Chicago. Once, my roommate and I got into my Toyota and started driving looking for a cafe and did not stop 'til we reached Greenwich Village."

Timing, as I said. I was well aware that San Francisco had been the place to be in 1968 when I got there 15 years later. But I was in the eighth grade in 1968. The idea of packing up at 13 and announcing to my machine operator father that I needed to move to an inspiring ambience more gratifying to my creative nature was out of the question. Or rather, the question did not yet exist. I did not even know then that I was made of the stuff of poets; I thought it was just me.

It seems that all my life, while my body is rooted to one place, my mind and spirit are drifting elsewhere, longing for other stomping grounds from which to knead new verses. So at 13 in the eighth grade I longed for my mother's hometown, a magical, magnificent unseen place about which she recounted to me over and over. The place of her childhood, her poverty and imagination. Her stepfather selling used books for a living on the corner for decades. Her mother playing the harmonica as she lay dying on a straw mat in the dark room in which the whole family lived. Mexico City.

At that time I nevertheless did not know that I had a hometown of my own—until

I moved away nearly two decades later.

But after five years of trying to make ends meet as one among an estimated 5,000 poets in the Bay area, I thought it might be practical to relocate once again. Instead, I chose an unlikely city in the Southwest far from having any kind of reputation for drawing the artistically-inclined, which serves more as refuge than cultural ambience for me.

In the three-hundred year old plaza I write on my lap beneath the winter desert sun. I realize now that a long time ago I learned to write poems anywhere. I'm here because this place just feels good...*to me*. Neruda said your home is where your books are. I've put up all my books in the built-in bookshelves in my study; they're not going anywhere anymore. So I guess I'm home.

Heading Home

May 1st, 1951, my first day here. Traded from Cleveland to Chicago, the first colored ball player ever to play for the Sox—the first in the whole city because the Cubs didn't have any black players yet, either. I didn't know anybody in town and it happens that, after coming to this strange city, to this new ballclub, I'm the first guy to bat. First pitch comes right over the plate and I hit a home run through center field. The people who wanted to boo me didn't get a chance. But later they got a chance. The bases were loaded and I was playing third base. A hit bounced off the bag and hit my ankle, then went through my legs. I was charged with an error, and two runs scored. My first game on the White Sox I was at the top and then sunk to the bottom. Same day, good and bad.

The summer went by, things on the field were mostly good, and I started to fall in love with the city because the people were so very good to me. No matter where I go, or what I do, after 1951, I always come back to Chicago, and am still involved with the White Sox organization, I think until the day I die—and I'm planning to live 100 years. Even when I went back to Cuba to play ball in the off-season, I still left most of my belongings right here. The love and respect I have for the organization and the fans of Chicago have been returned to me. Everybody knows me. The kids come up and say to me, "Minnie, I never saw you play but you're my idol—my grandfather saw you and told me all about how you played." Some treat me like I'm still playing—and there are days when I wish it was true.

I'm the kind of baseball player who had fun, always enjoyed the games and made good friends just about wherever I went. But let me tell you, if I played in the infield instead of outfield, I would have had even more fun. Once, a trick was played on me that I never forgot. It was against Detroit in 1956. I was having a great year but I had to fight for my life, getting hit by pitches, diving for balls. I was hobbling around on one leg by the end of the season, but I didn't want to sit out, no matter how bad it got, because I wanted to play in every single game. So I was banged up, but late in the game against Detroit, I got a hit and made it to first base as the tying run. The first baseman, Earl Torgeson, was a guy that never talked to me. I don't know why, because he had a group of guys he talked to—Nellie Fox, a few others—but to me, never a word—never. The pitcher takes a signal and I take a few steps

off the base…he throws over to first, trying to pick me off. "Safe," the ump says. Then Torgeson says to me, right in front of the ump, "Hey Minnie, please step off the base, I need to clean it." In my surprise, I just did what he asked. When I did, he tagged me and the ump said, "You're OUT." I told him there must be a misunderstanding—that he must be kidding. "Minnie, I told you, you're out. You shoulda asked for time-out." I said "Four-eyes, you heard it! He asked me to get off the base! He even said please!" Even as I yelled, I knew he was right. And Torgeson, I can't tell you exactly what I told him, but lets just say I told him to be careful. I went back to the dugout and the whole team got on me. Nellie said "Hey Mooch, whatsa matter? You gettin' tired? Needed to sit down?" I just asked him what does he want me to do? Kill the man? I was hot. The guy had fooled me.

Turns out Torgeson wasn't a bad guy, though. He came up to me next time we played and said he was sorry. He even told me to get a certain bat he was using that was doing his hitting some good. I ordered the bat and it helped me have a great season the following year. Maybe he knew that he was going to be traded to the Sox in '57. We got to be good friends, but for years, I think he felt bad about that trick he played on me. He was always worried that someday I was going to get back at him. I just let him sweat for awhile before I told him that revenge wasn't my way.

I can't tell you why it is that, with all the good games I had, most of the memories that stay in my head are of the times I made bad plays or had a tough day. But if I think about it long enough, and concentrate hard, I can remember the good days, the *Go Go White Sox*, the first great Comiskey Park, and the sounds of all the fans—and remember the feeling of running around those bases, headed for Home.

"The saloons can tell you a lot about a city, and it has nothing to do with the questions of sobriety."

CLARENCE PAGE

CLARENCE PAGE, JOURNALIST

Your Corner Saloon

Chicago's the kind of city where you can be born, grow up, get married, get a job, raise a family and die, all within five blocks. It's a working-class city. You don't realize what a working-class city is until you've lived somewhere else, like Washington D.C., where they don't have factories and they don't have corner saloons.

A part of Chicago's character is defined by the corner saloon. A friend of mine, a sociologist, spent a whole afternoon explaining to me the mysteries of neighborhood saloons, and the differences between the ones located on the corner, and the ones located in the middle of the block or on a commercial strip. There are real differences. Each of the different types says something about the nature of the neighborhood and the people who go there. The one that's on the corner is a combination social club, meeting hall, family reunion place and block headquarters. The saloon in the middle of the block, on the other hand, reduces its emphasis on socializing and increases its emphasis on drinking. And the saloon on the commercial strip is a different variety altogether, more of a cosmopolitan, "out on the town" kind of place, where the feel is less personal.

Saloons can tell you a lot about a city, and it has nothing to do with questions of sobriety. Instead, it has to do with social habits of tradition and culture. The saloon plays a central role in social networking, where it's more important *who* you know rather than *what* you know; the cities that don't have them tend to be less readily accessible to outsiders. In cities without neighborhood saloons, personal connections, or lack thereof, can decide whether you succeed or fail in life. In Chicago, you can walk into one of these joints and soon become part of the culture, part of the opportunity matrix.

And that's what is so amazing to me. I was a small-town kid from southern Ohio—came to Chicago with a duffel bag on my shoulder and was able to work my way right in with relative ease and become a Chicagoan. It's a city with arms open.

People tell me that when they come to Chicago, they find it a very friendly city, that people are eager to help, and that they tend to be much more courteous than, say, New Yorkers. That tells you something important: Chicagoans, no matter how rushed they are as they head off to work or down the block to their local saloon, more often than not, they'll take the time to mind their manners.

Flash Bulletin

I have never really let myself be simply cast as a sports announcer. If I have one thing going for me as a broadcaster, I think it's versatility, because I've done it all and I know how to do it all. Besides, when you get down to it, a sports guy would be the best man to start building a broadcast staff with, because he can ad-lib; he doesn't have to follow a script.

In the summer of 1944, Chicago was host to not one, but both, national political conventions. At that time, I was a broadcaster for WGN and the Mutual Radio Network, having moved from Peoria to Chicago four years prior, and was covering the events from the anchor booth. I had worked very hard to prepare for those conventions, and had pictures, biographies and histories of every important American politician and political figure, who could possibly be involved, and it really paid off. There are three important elements to a political convention: The nomination of the president, the nomination of the vice president, and finally, the adoption of the platform. In late June, at Chicago Stadium, the Republicans had accomplished the first two by nominating Dewey and Bricker. It was announced that the following day, at 4 p.m., the adoption of the party platform would take place, with a speech by one of the party's ranking members, Senator Robert Taft of Ohio. The other networks couldn't air the speech because they had committed to other shows, but Mutual decided to cover it live, beginning promptly at the stated time.

The following day, at 4 p.m., we take the air live, but our senator from Ohio is nowhere in sight. The only word we get is that he has left the hotel and is on his way to the Stadium. So I did what I had to do, I stalled. How do you hold an audience in a situation like this? We didn't really know where Taft was, or what had happened to him, so this is where homework by Brickhouse paid off, assisted further, maybe, by my experience as a sports broadcaster.

I had pertinent information and anecdotes about every important person there. Between interviews, I could watch the action on the floor, visually identifying the participants. "Here's California Governor Earl Warren talking to Senator Brooks of Illinois…and there's Harold Raineville, executive assistant to Congressman Everett Dirksen, talking with Tom Dewey's right-hand man." After all, Dewey had seriously considered Dirksen for vice president. It

JACK BRICKHOUSE, HALL OF FAME BROADCASTER

was like calling a ballgame. Of course, Senator Taft did finally show up, 50 minutes late, with some kind of excuse involving Chicago traffic—and presented the party platform.

But it was the Democrats, of course, who dominated presidential politics at that time, and, consequently, provided much more drama and political intrigue than the GOP could ever muster. Several weeks later, in July of 1944, again at Chicago Stadium, the Democrats gathered to nominate Franklin Roosevelt for his historic fourth term, and, simultaneously replace Vice President Henry Wallace with Harry Truman, the good, hard-nosed senator from Missouri—which is a story of epic consequences in itself because of the pivotal role in world history Truman would shortly play.

The War was very much on the minds of the delegates, and everyone was hungry for news, which traveled at a slightly slower clip in the era of pre-satellite technology. On July 20, 1944, a broadcast over the powerful Deutschlandsender radio station revealed that an assassination attempt had been made against Hitler, orchestrated by some of his own men. The world later learned that the attempt had been carried out by a one-eyed, one-armed colonel by the name of Klaus Von Stauffenberg, who, with a powerful time-bomb hidden in his briefcase, had narrowly missed his mark. The bomb had exploded at precisely 12:42 p.m. at "Wolf's Lair," Hitler's secret headquarters in the East Prussian forest, and it wasn't until more than six hours later that the news of the attempt was broadcast throughout Europe. It was early afternoon when the bulletin was received in our WGN newsroom here in Chicago and was immediately forwarded to us out at the Stadium. Jim Hanlon, our publicity director, got hold of it, and, being publicity-conscious, gave me the bulletin, told me to stand by, and went to see the chairman of the convention. Not five minutes later, I was at the podium delivering this very important news story to everyone, becoming, I was told, at the age of 28, the only broadcaster in United States history to address a national political convention. That was quite a moment.

Oh, there were many stories born at those conventions that summer. Did I tell you about Mayor Ed Kelly's close ties to the Roosevelt White House…?

"Ditka threw a block on Boyd that was so crushing it looked like a car wreck on the Dan Ryan. I swore I thought that Boyd's head was gonna wind up in Lake Michigan."

CHET COPPOCK

CHET COPPOCK, SPORTS COMMENTATOR

Full House

You gotta begin with this basic premise: I don't want to sound treasonistic, and I don't want to sound communistic, but in the arena of sports, wins and losses don't mean that much to me. I'm the kind of guy who likes big crowds, likes noise, loves the pure sex appeal of it all—the absolutely Picasso-like color of a tremendous crowd, a full house. What I love about Chicago, and the entire sports ambience of this town, is the excitement generated by an arena packed with people. For sheer electricity, for pure drama, you can't match Chicago Stadium for a big hockey game. Or when the Bulls are playing a big playoff game, that roar of the crowd. That feeling when you get 19,000 separate sets of vocal chords that almost become one. When it comes to sheer flavor for sports, Chicago delivers.

Generally speaking, there is no group quite like Bears fans. Those tickets are handed down from grandfathers to fathers to sons. I got to see every home game that Mike Ditka played in a Chicago Bear uniform. I remember the hit he made on Bobby Boyd (a defensive back for Baltimore) after Johnny Morris caught a pass and was headed downfield, in Wrigley Field in '62. Ditka threw a block on Boyd that was so crushing it looked like a car wreck on the Dan Ryan. I swore I thought that Boyd's head was gonna wind up in Lake Michigan. I had never seen a block so devastating in my entire life. Neither had the fans.

Chicago has also had the pleasure of witnessing two of the finest football players ever to play the game. Pound for pound, inch for inch, nobody comes close to Gale Sayers and Dick Butkus. As great a player as Walter Payton was, as a pure runner, he could not begin to compare to Gale Sayers. Keep in mind that he only played 68 games and still made the Hall of Fame, and was chosen a starter on the NFL's first 50 year team. That's how great this man was. Sayers was Baryshnikov in shoulder pads, Brando in *The Godfather*. He was the *elixir*—I mean, there was nothing quite like the guy. And he played in our town.

Two thoughts come to mind about Dick Butkus. One is seeing him for the first time as a rookie. He had that crew cut and that snarl; what a frighteningly imposing man he was. It was as if the Bears had called central casting and said, "Send us a football player." The second thing is that he's never been given the credit he deserved. He literally gave it his all, right up to the last game, when his knees finally gave out on him. Today, Dick walks with a very pronounced limp and he's bow-legged, but I honestly don't think it makes a damn bit of difference to him because all the man ever wanted to do was play football.

As for the fans' affection for their sports figures, I can't ever remember a town having a love affair with anybody the way this town had with Ernie Banks. Here's a guy who never played with a big winner. The bulk of his career was played with a bunch of guys who were out of the race before Mother's Day, if not sooner. But, this town loved Ernie.

He coined the phrase, "The Cubs Will Shine in '69," and Wrigley Field was just magical that year. I'd be hard-pressed to pick a sports event I've attended in Chicago and say that I've felt goose bumps the way I did on Opening Day, when Ernie Banks homered in his first two at-bats with 43,000 people in the stands. When Willie Smith came up to the plate in the bottom of the 12th and hit a home run into the right field bleachers, my God, I have never heard an ovation like that in my life. You would have sworn that the President had just made an 86 percent tax cut across the board. That game set the tone for the first six months of the '69 season. You could hardly wait to go to that ballpark because there was a different hero every day.

As far as any defining moment for Chicago fans, I recall vividly in '88 when the White Sox were on the verge of moving down to St. Petersburg. At the request of a White Sox board member, I served as emcee at a couple of "Save Our Sox" rallies in Daley Plaza. The attendance was not overwhelming; at the time the White Sox were very, very down. During one of the rallies, an electrical worker walked up to me and asked if he could just say a few words. I gave him an introduction and he got up there and said more in five words than Ernest Hemingway could have written in *The Old Man and the Sea*, or Michelangelo could have brushed with the most vivid colors imaginable. He talked about his father and his grandfather and what the White Sox meant to him. When he was finished, there wasn't a dry eye in the place. Chicago fandom has been depicted, all too often, as being Archie Bunker-like. And nothing could be further from the truth.

Chicago has also been blessed by a string of play-by-play announcers over the years who, whether you liked them or not, became an integral part of the event. Jack Brickhouse *was* Cubs' baseball. And, for almost a quarter of a century, he announced the Bears games with Irv Kupcinet. Kup had a great line about those years, "Well, Jack and I had done football for 24 years and there was only one problem. Jack and I were generally describing the game that was actually taking place on the field."

There is no town that delivers the goods like Chicago. There's no city in the world that's quite like this one from an anticipatory sense. This town will not buy a play-by-play man who doesn't root for the home team. There are some people who take a poke at Johnny Kerr because he would scream like a Gordon Tech cheerleader when Jordan went in for a slam dunk. But that's the beauty of Johnny Kerr. He doesn't have to tell fans all the details. Instead, he's roarin' with that gutteral explosion. It's like Gable saying to Vivian Leigh, "Frankly my dear, I don't give a damn." It couldn't be more appropriate.

People in this town are galvanized by sports, yet they're very accepting. I think it's characteristic of the way this town operates. It's not about winning or losing; it's all about ambience.

The Little Theater

It was autumn, close to November, and I was up at my parents' house in Winnetka. I had about one hour to deliver the artwork for a *Reader* ad to Joe Shannahan announcing my upcoming New Years Eve show at *The Metro*. There I was, driving breakneck into Evanston, parking illegally at the McDonalds, running into the Kinko's next door, still doing the math to try and figure out how to shrink my 8"x 11" page into the requisite 2"x 3" layout allotment. Right. So I muscle past the hordes of Northwestern students politely waiting in line till I nab some politely attending salesperson, and I swear under my breath until he does the math for me, and we crop and paste our way into a tidy little box which does nicely, and I whip out the door, pull the parking ticket off the windshield wiper and head for Lake Shore Drive.

Now, having lived for 16 years on the North Shore, I have driven this route so many times that it feels like my driveway. You bet I'm speeding, you bet I'm swearing. Who the fuck are these idiots in my driveway? I'm holding down the papers in the passenger seat with one hand, applying lipstick to my mouth with the other, and steering with my knee. Right. So I pop off at Irving and zoom towards Clark street. Left on Clark. Straight through the intersections, the lights are turning orange. It may be too late, it's five past the hour. I picture Bill Wyman looking down at his wristwatch and shaking his head. "All right, boys. Start the presses."

Of course, *The Metro* loading dock is full of cars and for a split second I contemplate looking for a space on the street… Right. Fuck it. I squeeze my auto onto the sidewalk and forget about it. "HELLO! HELLO THERE!" I'm pounding on the main doors till somebody lets me in (I don't know enough to walk through the record store). We hustle down the hall to the "secret elevator" and ride up to the Executive Offices. My escort sneaks a glance at my sweaty, rabid face and kindly looks away. I picture the elevator stalling and the *Reader* presses rolling while a bunch of heavy mechanics work to pry us out.

Ah! The cool white calm of Joe's office! The groovy artwork! The heaping pile of CD's! Even a few bottles of Dom Perignon! And the view… It must be nice for him to retreat from the melee of a *Saturday Night All Ages* show to this *Adult Contemporary* loft of an office. I'd live there. So we sit and talk, and everything's fine, of course. He sends the ad over by messenger and blessedly cuts me out of the loop. Business. I swear, sometimes I wonder how

I ever happen to involve myself in assignments to which I am clearly unsuited. But, it's water under the bridge and pretty soon we are talking about tropical vacations, Chicago winters, Costa Rican hospitality. Joe and I share Seasonal Affective Disorders and we are like squirrels burying nuts.

The patter winds down and I get up to go when Joe has a spark of inspiration. "Have you ever seen *The Little Theater*?" No, in fact I don't know what he's talking about. Apparently, there is a little auditorium up here on the fourth floor, rarely used, which dates back to the first part of the century when *The Metro* was a Swedish Citizens club, or something like that. He leads me down an unfinished hall. We make a couple of right turns, past crates and equipment, beyond the reach of electrical light. It is so dark that I'm getting nervous and I chirp, "Joe? Joe?" every once in a while to make sure he's still up there. We come to these double doors and Joe pushes them open. I am suddenly standing at the entrance to a very large space of which I can see nothing, but can feel the depth and height and hear our voices reverberate against the far walls. Joe is fumbling around behind the door, looking for the light switch. It isn't working. "Hang on," he says, "Lemme go make sure the circuit is on." So Joe leaves me standing there at the mouth of an inky abyss, alone with time to think about it. In a weird way, the room is cool and attractive, a bit musty, but almost charged with its own emptiness. I squint and try to see into the darkness. All that my rods and cones can register is this super fast, frenetic movement of nothingness, like the flitting of gnats in a night sky. Then all of a sudden, what I had taken to be the product of a straining optical nerve slows down, and damn near stops to the left of me. My hair stood on end.

I felt the presence of somebody watching, somebody checking me out. The very first image to flash through my mind was that of an eight or nine-year-old girl, agitated by the interruption and simply coming to roost nearby to appraise me. I felt the abrupt need to ask her permission to be there.

Okay—this is freaky, right? But my imagination is so active that I am frequently visited by cinematic notions and I don't take them too seriously, I just go with the event at hand. So I silently asked to be welcome, explaining myself as a musician and a girl, who had come to take a look at the room, and would it be okay if I played here sometime? I pictured her kind of hesitant, suspicious but curious, much the same way a real girl would be around a woman of my age, wanting to make a friend, but feeling out the bogacity of my intent. I played it cool and waited. It reminded me of this *Sally Jesse Raphael* show I saw once in Florida, where a camera crew and a psychic were invited down to the restricted areas of the QEII to assess the validity of reported hauntings. They were walking around in this big, dark, echoey chamber (the old swimming pool) talking to the spirit of a young girl who could not find her mother. She cried out pitifully (and was duly recorded on tape) as she raced around the farthest walls, her voice tiny and pathetic, moving from one place to the next with terrifying, supernatural speed. The psychic was trying to calm her down, telling her that she didn't have to stay there, that her mommy was waiting for her on the other side of the light and that she shouldn't be afraid to go to her. The little voice was almost hysterical and the ship's crewman who was hosting the expedition was clearly horrified by the implications. I was as powerfully affected by the loneliness I heard as by the psychokinetic manifestation, true or not. It is horrible to find a child abandoned.

Well, my little spectre gave me the once over and a go ahead just in time for Joe to return and flip the lights on. I didn't say anything, of course, because I never say anything when strange feelings grip me, except to my girlfriends, who are understanding and excited by a good spooky tale. The stage was crowded with amplifiers which belonged to *The Smashing Pumpkins* and were being stored here while they toured overseas. Cool. The seats were red velvet and the back wall had electric candles that flickered in that kitschy, electric way. I would love to play here, I said. We returned to Joe's office and said goodbye.

A month later, I was in Los Angeles, playing a few shows. I heard *Urge* was there so I scammed my way into their afterhours gig at the *Viper Room*. I'm plowing through the hipsters clogging the bar, when I run into my friend, Tom, who was the manager of the record store at *Metro*. Wow! Hey! Cool to see you. It was hard to chat and *Urge* was about to go on, but we got in a bit of gab and I told him that I'd been up to see *The Little Theater* and I was looking forward to playing there sometime.

He leaned in all conspiratorially at the mention of that theater and said, "Do you know about *The Little Theater*?" I looked at him and got the goosebumps.

It's haunted, I thought to myself. "It's haunted!" he said.

It's a little girl, I thought to myself. "It's a little girl," said Tom.

JUAN RAMIREZ, ACTOR AND ARTISTIC DIRECTOR, LATINO CHICAGO THEATER

The Sun Piercing Through the Clouds

I grew up in Humboldt Park and was involved in gangs for a long time. One of my friends, Mexican Tony, had a rough childhood. His father beat him when he was a kid, and he used to sleep in hallways. He joined the army when he got old enough, and came back a heroin junkie. But Tony was a special guy with a great sense of humor—really intelligent, with a big heart. He was my friend.

I survived getting shot and spending a little time in jail, and was living outside of the neighborhood with my wife, who was nine months pregnant. We were really broke and lived in a basement apartment, where we slept on a mattress on the floor. I was working part-time and taking theater classes at night. In my free time I would try to organize in my old neighborhood. Basketball leagues, mural projects, block parties…

In 1980, two days before our big summer block party, Tony was stabbed in the chest. He died on the way to the hospital.

We dedicated the block party to his memory, and the whole thing went off without incident. Usually, there were at least a few fistfights, but not this year. On the bus ride home, I couldn't stop thinking about my friend, Tony, about how difficult his life had been.

When I got home my wife was awake. She was lying there in the dark. I asked her what was the matter and she said she didn't feel too well, her stomach slightly upset. I asked her if she wanted to call the hospital and she said she didn't think it was necessary, but we walked to the corner and called anyway. They told us to come in and we called a taxi, but it didn't come. So we got on the bus.

There wasn't any sense of urgency and we were both pretty wiped out at 5 a.m. so the bus ride was pretty quiet. I couldn't stop thinking about Tony.

When we got to the hospital, the nurses took my wife, and I filled out the paperwork. When I finished, I went upstairs to the maternity ward. As I got off the elevator, I heard a slap—and then crying. My first son had been born. It was at that moment that I realized we couldn't affect the past, and that, if we weren't careful, we would miss the present and lose the future. I named my son Tony Antonio Abalcab Ramirez. And I feel both Tonys very strongly. Even though they're not always around.

No Observable Diminution

According to Carl Sandburg's poem of 1916, Chicago was the "stormy, husky, brawling, City of the Big Shoulders," and, more to the point, "Hog Butcher for the World." Chicago, of course, was the center of the meat packing industry in the United States, from just after the Civil War until World War II. At the center of this activity was the Chicago Stockyards. The animals, primarily cattle, were brought in live, most often by train, and were placed in enormous holding pens in the stockyards until they were slaughtered. The wooden pens in which the animals were kept had bins containing feed and corn. The stockyard conditions in general, but, particularly, the plentiful feed, attracted a monumental number of common pigeons, which fed on the spilled grains and the animal droppings. They built nests from various scraps—including wood, straw, pieces of glass, and old, oily rags—and tucked them into every spare nook and cranny. Consequently, for most of its history, the stockyards were afflicted with fires, some of which were very large and ruinous. I can recall when I came to Chicago in 1939, fires in the "Yards" were a common occurrence, with at least one major blaze every summer. The birds not only were the indirect cause of these fires, but they carried germs and diseases that could directly affect the health of the stockyard animals. Worse yet, their numbers seemed to be ever escalating.

The owners of the stockyards tried to devise a scheme to control this very real pest. Their solution was the "Chicago Stockyards Pigeon Shoot," which was organized by the president of the Stockyards, William Wood Prince. He assembled a group of 30 or 40 individuals who were expert shotgun shooters to help control the pigeon population in the area. We would shoot on a Sunday morning, once a month. After we shot the birds, sometimes as many as 2,000, they would be picked up, put in sacks, and placed by the massive graystone entrance to the stockyards. Before long, the sacks would be taken away, and I suppose the birds were boiled and eaten for dinner.

The Stockyards Shoot had a real mixture of people. On one hand, were Leon Mandel and his world champion marksman wife, Carola, along with a number of other business people from Chicago, including Marshall Field IV. Also present, were managers of gun shops, a number of truck drivers, radio personalities, ex-policeman and a variety of others.

The common denominator was that they all liked to shoot, and they were good shots. The birds were extremely difficult to kill; pigeons fly very rapidly, and once a shot was fired, they usually swerved or dived, forcing a difficult second shot. The shoot took place under the supervision of the Chicago Police, including the head of the detail, Captain Tom Reynolds. Squad cars patrolled the area during the shoot, which normally started at 10 a.m. and lasted until just after noon. Each shooter was given an identifying red kerchief to wear around his or her neck, because there were a number of other individuals who would have volunteered to participate. It was a distinct privilege to be invited to participate in the shoot.

Sunday morning was the time chosen because it was the period of minimum activity in the yards. There were no receipts, no deliveries, and only a small number of people working around the area. A principal concern of the activity was to insure that the shooters didn't harm any person or animal, nor damage any of the facilities. Therefore, it was necessary to have individuals who knew how to handle a gun. After the shoot was completed, we would all adjourn to the Stockyards Inn at 43rd and Halsted and enjoy a huge luncheon, swapping stories from the day's shoot. Even though the number of pigeons killed each month was high, the birds bred so fast that there seemed to be absolutely no diminution—no observable diminution, anyway—in their supply.

Those of us who participated in the Stockyards Shoot enjoyed it for a number of years, from the early '50s until the Yards shut down in 1971, when it had become obvious that it was cheaper to slaughter animals in Kansas, Nebraska, Oklahoma and Texas, and ship the finished product, rather than ship live animals. Of course, when the Stockyards moved out of Chicago, the birds virtually disappeared from that particular area, though most of them seemed simply to move their home down to the Chicago Public Library. In any case, the "Chicago Stockyards Pigeon Shoot" was a unique activity in the history of Chicago that, at the very least, attempted to serve a very real purpose.

"There's an expression that God writes straight with crooked lines, and I think that's a hallmark of real Christianity…"

FATHER GEORGE CLEMENTS

FATHER GEORGE CLEMENTS, CATHOLIC PRIEST, SOCIAL ACTIVIST

God's Mysterious Ways

Holy Angels Church suffered the misfortune of burning to the ground in 1986 with the help of an electrical short. The parish has come a long way since then.

This area is, in fact, the lowest socio-economic area in the city of Chicago, this is *real* poverty, this is *the* ghetto. To have a new church built here—the only one in the world that is heated and air-conditioned with solar energy—is intriguing.

I've bragged for years that you can look around this neighborhood and find plenty of buildings with graffiti on them, yet nobody ever puts graffiti on our walls. It's because people really do look upon this parish as something unusual and unique, and something which should be preserved. We have a wall in the playground behind the church we call the "Wall of Roots," a painted mural that has been here for almost 20 years. It's weatherbeaten now, but it portrays various African themes, from the slave ships coming to America and the southern cotton plantations, to black heroes such as Harriet Tubman, Booker T. Washington, Malcolm X, and Dr. King. It encourages the idea that knowledge and education are the keys to success in life. Our school, adjacent to the church, has an overflowing enrollment of 1,300 students, all of whom have a strong respect for that wall; when they are out there playing, and some kid misses the ball and it hits the wall, it's serious business. It's as if the wall itself has become sacred. I think some of that same sacred quality has been transferred to the new church; people treat it with a very special care and respect.

Skidmore, Owings & Merrill, the architectural firm responsible for the Sears Tower, designed our church; it certainly isn't something one would expect to find here along East Oakwood Boulevard. Inside the church are the monumental mural of the Holy Angels, the bronze sculpture by Richard Hunt and the beautiful stained glass by Roy Lichtenstein.

So how did this church of the 21st century get built in one of Chicago's most blighted areas? There's an expression that God writes straight with crooked lines, and I think that's a hallmark of real Christianity, that there are all kinds of strange, inexplicable things that can happen…

Big City

Since the age of 15, I'd been a pretty damn good waitress. As good as I was though, I knew I didn't want to be one the rest of my life. I grew up in the town of Ironwood, Michigan, where I accepted the expected employment dreams of small-town Catholic girls, at various times wanting to become a beautician, a model, even a nun. Yet clearly, my early calling was waitressing. I understood it not solely as a means of income, but as a way to experience and interact with—really to begin to understand—a wide range of people. Waitressing supported me through my years of high school in Ironwood, and college in Kalamazoo. It even followed me, briefly, to the *Big City*.

In June of 1969, with a fresh degree in biology and a minor in chemistry, I arrived in Chicago to find a job. I spent most of the first day overwhelmed by traffic. I wouldn't say that I had a definitive plan, just some scattered ideas: Maybe I would find a job at a bakery or a bread factory where I could act as a chemist, checking procedures and ingredients. Or maybe there was a job for me at one of the medical schools as a lab technician, checking (or cleaning) petri dishes. Or maybe, just maybe, there was a job for me in the serene suburbs at Abbott Labs, where the grass was nice and green, and the trees were big and healthy. I just wasn't convinced I was ready to live amidst the asphalt and bricks, the stone and steel. But I was offered a job at Northwestern Memorial Hospital in their immunology lab, and, on the day Neil Armstrong walked on the moon, I moved into my first Chicago apartment near Belmont and Broadway. The girl upstairs threw a moonwalk party and I took one small step towards becoming a Chicagoan.

Patterson was in charge of the lab. Immediately, he realized he had hired somewhat of an overachiever. I had been hired as a technician, but, upon arrival, wanted to co-write academic papers with all of the physicians who were there doing research. I also got very involved with the patients who were participating in the research projects, constantly talking to them and getting a sense of how they were doing—even driving them back and forth when they couldn't make it on their own. The medical environment appealed to me intensely. I didn't have any money for med school, but, for the second time in my life, I was being called. As tentative as I initially was about urban life, I got hooked fast. When the

DR. RENEE HARTZ, CHIEF OF CARDIOTHORACIC SURGERY, UNIVERSITY OF ILLINOIS AT CHICAGO

decision had to be made about where to apply to school, I knew I wouldn't consider leaving Chicago.

More than two decades later, I have that same feeling. I've been offered positions at many hospitals, but if they were beyond the city limits, I rarely gave a second look. Even a hospital in San Diego made overtures, and the thought of consistently beautiful weather did hold some appeal. But there is something about Chicago, related to its intemperate climate or not, that promotes a nose-to-the-grindstone productivity that is more suited to my nature. Building a self-sufficient and competitive heart surgery program from scratch here at the University of Illinois at Chicago on West Taylor Street might sound like a lot of work—or even an impossible task—to some people. But to these ears, and this mind, it sounds like a tremendous challenge. And if there's one thing that can inspire a Chicagoan, whether they're from Ironwood or Chicago, it's a challenge.

"I went to see Arthur about it. He was very ill by this time, fighting cancer. 'Don't do it, don't do it. I've lost enough friends already.' He couldn't see that this was something that I *had* to do. I felt I no longer had any choice. "

BILL PINKNEY

BILL PINKNEY, SAILOR

Against the Wind

In 1974, after a stint in the service, the company I was working for on the East Coast sent me back to the city in which I had grown up, the city to which I had vowed never to return. I found myself living at Lakeview and Wrightwood, not far from the area my sister and I used to call "Never-Never Land."

It was a short distance to Belmont Harbor and I often went over just to be around the boats. If you're a person with sailing in your blood, and you don't have a vessel of your own, you have to find other ways to get out there on the water. My way was to figure out which boats I wanted to sail on, find out who owned them, and hitch a ride by offering to crew.

There was one boat, in particular, that caught my attention: a PJ-43, a Palmer-Johnson, designed by a company in Sturgeon Bay, Wisconsin, and built in Finland. I met a guy named Josh Ruterburg, who took care of it for the owner, and would often go over to talk sailing with him. One day, we were by the boat shooting the breeze, when the owner pulled up in his big Lincoln. I told Josh I'd see him later. I went to my car, which was parked close by, and got in and waited, just to see what the guy looked like. The owner got out of his car, walked over to the boat and said a few words to Josh, then turned around and walked straight toward me. He tapped on the passenger side window and I opened the door for him. He got in and just looked at me. "What's with the beard?" was his first question. And then, "Are you a sailor? Are you any good?" and, "Want to go sailing Saturday at noon?" I just looked at him and nodded. He opened the door to leave, and then, realized what he'd forgotten. "The name's Arthur Dickholtz," and he shook my hand.

My first day sailing with Arthur was a miserable one. Foggy, rainy and colder than it needed to be, the rudder control broke and we had to abandon the trip.

I sailed with Arthur from 1974 until he retired from the sport in the early '80s. He was my mentor. While racing, we used to argue at the top of our lungs about tactics. But the hollering never affected our friendship. He owned Flash Cabs, so maybe he felt he needed a gruff exterior in order to do business. Deep down, though, he was a man who would give you the shirt off his back.

It was in 1977 that I bought my first boat and started to sail alone. I did it not because

I didn't want to sail with other people anymore, but because I wanted to sail more often. I lived so close to the harbor, I wanted to be able to go out on the spur of the moment, something I couldn't do if I needed a crew. Over the next few years, I sailed more and more by myself, gradually gaining the confidence to venture further and further away. By the time I did the Trans-Lake race—152 miles—there was no holding me back. People started to tell me that, given what they knew of me, I would soon need to face a challenge that was beyond Lake Michigan; it was nothing short of a solo trip around the world. And for years, I denied that I had that kind of need. Finally, in 1985, I started to come to grips with the fact that my sailing friends were right.

I went to see Arthur about it. He was very ill by this time, fighting cancer. "Don't do it, don't do it. I've lost enough friends already." He couldn't see that this was something that I *had* to do. I felt I no longer had any choice. He died before I even started the trip. But if there was anyone who I would have liked to have been in Boston Harbor to witness my return, it was Arthur Dickholtz. He meant that much to me.

The irony of me making a journey around the world, and being welcomed into different ports around the world is, in my mind, so very clear. As children, my sister and I were up early on Sunday mornings in order to catch the Michigan Avenue bus from the South Side to its end-of-the-line on the northern end, Randolph Street. From there, we transferred to the Sheridan Road bus, a double-decker, which took us further north, through Lincoln Park and past the harbors. It was "Never-Never Land" to us because black kids weren't welcome there. We could see all of the beautiful wooden boats—no fiberglass yet in the late '40s and early '50s—but could never get too close. All we could do was watch them blur by.

When I sailed into ports around the world, I was welcomed as an American. Outside of this country, people are recognized for their nation of origin, not their ancestor's. It is only when I am in the United States that I become hyphenated, along with everyone else. Chicago has changed in that I can now live in a place that was once off-limits. I look forward to the day when we can all shed our hyphenated distinctions.

"Our city is street-wise and alley-hip of the casually familiar. Thus the Standard Oil Building and the John Hancock are, with tavern gaminess, referred to as Big Stan and Big John. Sears is simply that; never mind Roebuck."

STUDS TERKEL

STUDS TERKEL, WRITER AND RADIO HOST

Chicago

Janus, the two-faced god, has both blessed and cursed the city-state Chicago. Though his graven image is not visible to the naked eye, his ambiguous spirit soars atop Sears, Big Stan, and Big John. (Our city is street-wise and alley-hip of the casually familiar. Thus the Standard Oil Building and the John Hancock are, with tavern gaminess, referred to as Big Stan and Big John. Sears is simply that; never mind Roebuck. Ours is a one-syllable town. Its character has been molded by the muscle rather than the word.)

Our double-vision, double-standard, double-value, and double-cross have been patent ever since—at least, ever since the earliest of our city fathers took the Pottawattomies for all they had. Poetically, these dispossessed natives dubbed this piece of turf *Chikagou*. Some say it is Indian lingo for "City of the Wild Onion"; some say it really means "City of the Big Smell." "Big" is certainly the operative word around these parts.

Nelson Algren's classic, *Chicago: City on the Make* is the late poet's single-hearted vision of his town's doubleness. "Chicago… forever keeps two faces, one for winners and one for losers; one for hustlers and one for squares… One face for Go-Getters and one for Go-Get-It-Yourselfers. One for poets and one for promoters… One for early risers, one for evening hiders."

It is the city of Jane Addams, settlement worker, and Al Capone, entrepreneur; of Clarence Darrow, lawyer, and Julius Hoffman, judge; of Louis Sullivan, architect, and Sam Insull, magnate; of John Altgeld, governor, and Paddy Bauler, alderman. (Paddy's the one who some years ago observed, "Chicago ain't ready for reform.") And it's clear whose name among these has become the Chicago hallmark.

In a Brescian trattoria, to Italy's north, a wisp of an old woman, black shawl and all, hears where I'm from. Though she has some difficulty with English (far less than I have with Italian), she thrusts both hands forward, index fingers pointed at me: *Boom, boom,* she goes. I hold up my hands. We both laugh. It appears that Jimmy Cagney, Edward G. Robinson, and Warner Brothers have done a real job in image making.

Not that Al and his colleagues didn't have palmy days during what, to others, were parlous times. Roaring Twenties or Terrible Thirties, the goose always hung high for the

Boys. I once asked a casual acquaintance, the late Doc Graham, for a resume. Doc was, as he modestly put it, a dedicated heist man. His speech was a composite of Micawber and Runyon:

"The unsophisticated either belonged to the Bugs Moran mob or the Capone mob. The fellas with talent didn't belong to either one. We robbed both."

Wasn't that a bit on the risky side?

"Indeed. There ain't hardly a one of us survived the Biblical threescore and ten. You see this fellow liquidated, that fellow—shall we say, disposed of? Red McLaughlin was the toughest guy in Chicago. But when you seen Red run out of the drainage canal, you realized Red's *modus operandi* was unavailing. His associates was Clifford and Adams. They were set in Al's doorway in his hotel in Cicero. That was unavailing."

Was it a baseball bat Al used?

"You are doubtless referring to Anselmi and Scalisi. They offended Al. This was rare. Al Capone usually sublet the matter. Since I'm Irish, I had a working affiliate with Bugs Moran. Did you know that Red and his partners once stole the Checker Cab Company. They took machine guns, went up, and had an election. I assisted in that operation."

What role did the forces of law and order play?

"If you had a speaking acquaintance with the Mayor (Big Bill Thompson), you could do no wrong. Al spoke loud to him."

Yet years hence…as for the boy who stepped off the day coach at the La Salle Street depot on that August day, 1920, he has come to know, ever so slightly, the nature of the Roman god who, fable tells us, guards the gates of heaven. He knows, too, that the spirit of this god hovers over Chicago. He further knows that Janus, two-headed, has, of course, two forked tongues. So the boy, in the ultimate, knows that, despite the song, he'll not find Eden here. Here, in Chicago, this cock-eyed wonder of a town, he is—and all of us are—twice blessed and twice deceived. And he'll settle for that.

Biographies

Joseph Cardinal Bernardin Archbishop of Chicago since 1982, general secretary of the executive committee of the National Conference of U.S. Bishops, and member of the permanent council of the World Synod of Bishops. Widely respected within the Catholic community as a voice of reason and intellect. *Photographed in the Archdiocesan Pastoral Center.* (Chapter **30**)

Jack Brickhouse Journalist and sports broadcaster. Inducted into the Baseball Hall of Fame in Cooperstown in 1983 for his 5,300 games as the Chicago Cubs play-by-play announcer for WGN Television. *Photographed inside Chicago Stadium.* (Chapter **52**)

Gwendolyn Brooks Poet, writer. In 1950, won the Pulitzer Prize for her book of poems, *Annie Allen*, becoming the first black author to receive the award. Since 1968, she has been Poet Laureate of Illinois, succeeding the first Poet Laureate, Carl Sandburg. She has been awarded more than 50 honorary degrees, and, in 1994, received the federal government's highest honor for distinguished intellectual achievement in the humanities when she was invited to give the Jefferson Lecture in the Humanities. *Photographed outside of the Chicago Authors Room on the seventh floor of the Harold Washington Library.* (Chapter **21**)

Ana Castillo Poet, writer. In addition to being a widely published poet, is a novelist, essayist, translator, editor, teacher, and painter, and has won numerous awards for both her poetry and fiction. She is the author of several books, *Women are Not Roses, My Father Was a Toltec, The Mixquiahuala Letters, Sapogonia, and So Far From God*, among them. A non-fiction work, *Massacre of the Dreamers: Essays on Xicanisma* was published by the University of New Mexico Press in 1994. *Photographed in a North Milwaukee Avenue bookstore.* (Chapter **49**)

Fr. George Clements Catholic priest and community activist, pastor of Holy Angels Parish from 1969-1991. Founder of the *One Church—One Child* program, which is dedicated to finding Black adoptive parents for Black and bi-racial children. In 1981, he became the first Catholic priest to adopt a son; he has since adopted three more sons. Fr. Clements has dedicated his life to improving the lives of those less fortunate. *Photographed in front of Holy Angels Church.* (Chapter **57**)

Marva Collins Educator and founder of Westside Preparatory School. Subject of huge national media attention for her unorthodox ways of teaching and reaching inner-city children. Was offered the post of Secretary of Education by two presidents, but each time chose to continue her primary work with young students and their teachers. Recipient of countless education awards and honorary degrees. *Photographed at Westside Preparatory School.* (Chapter **41**)

Chet Coppock Former host of *Coppock on Sports*, previously the #1 radio sports talk show in America according to *USA Today*. Known for his glowing introductions of the show's guests, he is regarded as an authority in the world of Chicago sports. *Photographed at the Northwest corner of Soldier Field.* (Chapter **53**)

Denise DeClue Writer of articles, plays, and film scripts that are concerned with social issues and changing manners and mores. Denise has recently founded a production company, Flat-Iron Films, with her husband, Robert Schneiger, and they are working together on several documentary projects. *Photographed under the El near Nelson Algren's old apartment on West Evergreen Street.* (Chapter **18**)

Roger Ebert Film critic. Since 1967 has written movie reviews for the *Chicago Sun-Times*, reviews which are currently distributed to more than 200 other newspapers. He is the co-host of *Siskel & Ebert*, the long-running nationally syndicated television program. The only motion picture critic to have won the Pulitzer Prize for distinguished criticism (1975), he has been a Lecturer on Film for the University of Chicago Extension Division since 1969. *Photographed under the El at the corner of Wabash and Lake Streets.* (Chapter **40**)

Dr. Lester Fisher Retired director of the Lincoln Park Zoo, the oldest and most widely attended zoo in the country. Prior to replacing Marlin Perkins as director, he served for 15 years as the zoo's consulting veterinarian. During his tenure as director (1962-1992), Dr. Fisher shifted the zoo's focus increasingly toward conservation and education. *Photographed in the McCormick Bird House at the Lincoln Park Zoo.* (Chapter **36**)

Aaron Freeman Comedian, political satirist, writer, producer, actor, and host. This *Second City* alumnus is as comfortable with comedy—as he proved in his theater shows, *Do the White Thing*, and *Disguised as a Grown-Up*—as he is with conversation and analysis, which he proves weekly with *Talking with Aaron Freeman*, a television talk show for WPWR, and *Metropolis*, a four-hour Saturday radio program for *WBEZ*. *Photographed on the roof of a North Milwaukee Avenue Building.* (Chapter **15**)

Dean Grazier Lifelong Cub fan, Wrigley Field employee from 1966-1991. When he retired, he was charged with the duties of head scorekeeper in the only manually-changed scoreboard left in Major League Baseball. *Photographed in the Wrigley Field scoreboard.* (Chapter **1**)

b

Buddy Guy Legendary blues guitarist who influenced a wide range of fellow guitarists including Jimi Hendrix, Carlos Santana, and Eric Clapton. He won a Grammy Award for his 1992 album, *Damn Right, I've Got the Blues*, and, in 1993, received Billboard Magazine's highest honor, the *Century Award*, for distinguished creative achievement. *Photographed in his South Wabash blues club, Legends.* (Chapter **9**)

Daryl Hannah Actress. Began her acting studies at The Goodman Theater; won early praise for her tender and terrifying performance as "Pris," the murderous but vulnerable *replicant* in Ridley Scott's *Blade Runner*. Since then, she has appeared in many feature films including *Splash, Roxanne, Steel Magnolias, At Play in the Fields of the Lord*, and the science fiction satire *Attack of the Fifty-Foot Woman*, which she co-produced. She heads her own production company, Reel Fias Co., which currently has several feature film projects in development. *Photographed outside of The Museum of Science and Industry.* (Chapter **31**)

Dr. Renee Hartz Chief of Cardiothoracic Surgery at University of Illinois Hospital at Chicago and Professor of Surgery in the Cardiothoracic Surgery Division of University of Illinois at Chicago. Nationally known as a leader in her field and a pioneer of new technologies. Her writings relating to heart surgery have been widely published in books and medical journals. *Photographed in front of University of Illinois Hospital.* (Chapter **58**)

Christie Hefner Chairman and chief executive officer of Playboy Enterprises, Inc. Daughter of Hugh Hefner, the founder of *Playboy Magazine*, she has transformed the once struggling media giant into a thriving, international, diversified media and entertainment company. *Photographed in Playboy's North Lake Shore Drive Headquarters.* (Chapter **11**)

Nicole Hollander Creator of the nationally syndicated cartoon strip, "Sylvia," which appears in more than 70 newspapers including the *Chicago Tribune*, the *Boston Globe*, and the *Los Angeles Times*. *Photographed near her North Side office.* (Chapter **10**)

Ben Hollis Television producer and performer; widely known as the former producer, host, and co-creator of WTTW's hit series, *Wild Chicago*, for which he earned three Emmy Awards. A graduate of *The Players Workshop of Second City*, he has performed as a comedian, improv actor, and singer/songwriter around the Chicagoland area since 1978. *Photographed in front of 950 West Wrightwood.* (Chapter **43**)

Jesse Jackson Social activist and political figure, increasingly active in international affairs; in addition, a shadow senator for the District of Columbia, host of a talk show for CNN, and founder of Operation PUSH (People United to Save Humanity) and the Rainbow Coalition. He made two bids for the Democratic presidential nomination, in 1984 and 1988. His autobiography is *A Time to Speak* (1988). *Photographed in his Washington, D.C., office.* (Chapter **19**)

Helmut Jahn President and CEO of Murphy/Jahn; architect of international acclaim, acknowledged as one of the ten most influential living American architects. Well-known in Chicago for the James R. Thompson Center and the United Airlines Terminal 1 Complex at O'Hare Airport, both of which have received worldwide attention. Complementing Murphy/Jahn's main office in Chicago are its branch offices in Munich and Frankfurt. *Photographed at his desk in his Chicago office.* (Chapter **22**)

Dr. Mae Jemison Astronaut. On September 12, 1992, served aboard the shuttle *Endeavour* as Science Mission Specialist, thus becoming the first African-American woman to go into space. A chemical engineer, scientist, physician, and astronaut, is also well-versed in the areas of computer programming, nuclear resonance spectroscopy, reproductive biology and tropical medicine. Dr. Jemison has recently founded The Jemison Group, which researches, creates, and markets advanced technologies for the developing world. Its first project is the development of a satellite-based telecommunication system to improve health care in West Africa. *Photographed in front of the Art Institute of Chicago on South Michigan Avenue.* (Chapter **6**)

John H. Johnson Founded, in 1942, the Johnson Publishing Company, which has become a business empire. In addition to publishing *Ebony, Jet and EM* magazines, the company manufactures beauty products, produces television shows, and owns several radio stations. *Photographed in his office at company headquarters.* (Chapter **44**)

Tim Kazurinsky Screenwriter and actor, performed with *The Second City* and was a cast member and writer for *Saturday Night Live*. Movie appearances include *Neighbors, Shakes the Clown*, and three *Police Academy* films. He wrote (with Denise DeClue) the screenplays for *About Last Night...* and *For Keeps*. *Photographed on the corner of Wabash and Randolph.* (Chapter **17**)

Ardis Krainik General Director of the world-renowned Lyric Opera of Chicago which is known for its innovative and visually stunning productions of classical and modern operas. For the past six seasons, Lyric has exceeded 101 percent of capacity, a record unequalled in the performing arts world. *Photographed in the Grand Foyer of the Civic Opera House.* (Chapter **48**)

Irv Kupcinet Author of "Kup's Column" for the *Chicago Sun-Times* since 1944. One-time NFL player and game official, subsequently broadcasted Chicago Bears football games with Jack Brickhouse for 25 years. Hosted *Kup's Show*, a television talk show, for 27 years. Considered a journalistic institution; In 1986, the Wabash Avenue Bridge was officially renamed the "Irv Kupcinet Bridge." *Photographed in his Sun-Times office.* (Chapter **32**)

b

Bob Love All-Star basketball player for the Chicago Bulls from 1968-1977; known as "Butterbean." His scoring was so prodigious that the Bulls' scoring record he set wasn't touched until Michael Jordan claimed it in 1990. In 1994, he became only the second Chicago Bull to have his jersey retired. After leaving the Bulls as a player, Mr. Love overcame a severe stuttering problem that had diminished his post-basketball prospects. He currently serves as the Bulls' Director of Community Relations. *Photographed on West Madison Street.* (Chapter **38**)

Sid Luckman Hall of Fame Bears quarterback, played from 1939 to 1950. Voted All-Pro eight times and Most Valuable Player three times. Became the first to attempt and master the George Halas innovation of the T-formation offense. Regarded as one of the ten "All-Time Great" National Football League quarterbacks. *Photographed at Wrigley Field.* (Chapter **33**)

Sophie Madej Proprietress of Sophie's Busy Bee Restaurant, a neighborhood establishment located directly across from Wicker Park on Damen Avenue, which was featured prominently in National Geographic's May, 1991, issue about Chicago. A great believer in the strength of urban neighborhoods, she draws from her own experience gleaned from a brief stint in the suburbs: "Nobody knew nobody, and everybody knew everything." *Photographed in the kitchen of the Busy Bee.* (Chapter **14**)

Amy Madigan Stage and screen actress, known for her roles as the angry daughter *Sonny* in Bud Yorkin's film *Twice in a Lifetime* with Gene Hackman and Ellen Burstyn, and as Kevin Costner's sensible wife in *Field of Dreams*. Among many other stage credits, she co-starred with Jessica Lange in the Broadway production of *A Streetcar Named Desire*. *Photographed in her dressing room at the Ethel Barrymore Theater in New York.* (Chapter **35**)

John Mahoney Versatile actor, known for his work in film, television, and on the stage. Screen work includes *Tin Men, Moonstruck, Frantic, Eight Men Out, Say Anything, The Russia House,* and *Barton Fink*. As a member of the famed Steppenwolf Theater he has appeared on their stage in nearly 30 productions, as well as guesting at theaters all over Chicago including The Body Politic, Northlight, and The Goodman. In 1986, Mr. Mahoney won a Tony Award for his work on Broadway in *The House of Blue Leaves*. On television, he plays Kelsey Grammer's down-to-earth father on the series, *Frasier*. *Photographed on the stage of the Steppenwolf Theater.* (Chapter **12**)

David Mamet Writer, director, screenwriter, and playwright. For the latter, he is known for *American Buffalo, Speed the Plow, Oleanna,* and Pulitzer Prize-winning *Glengarry Glen Ross*. Screenplays include *The Postman Always Rings Twice, The Verdict,* and *The Untouchables*. In addition, for the screen, he wrote and directed *House of Games, Homicide, Glengarry Glen Ross,* and *Hoffa*. *Photographed in his writing office in Cambridge, Massachusetts.* (Chapter **13**)

Joe Mantegna Actor, founding member of The Organic Theater. Conceived, co-wrote and in 1977 co-starred in the original staging of *Bleacher Bums*, the long-lived play based on his own experiences in the outfield seats of Wrigley Field's Friendly Confines. Screen credits include *House of Games, Queen's Logic, Homicide, Godfather III,* and *Searching for Bobby Fisher*. *Photographed near the corner of Sheffield and Waveland.* (Chapter **4**)

Abraham Lincoln Marovitz Senior Federal Judge, has lived a rich and colorful life worthy of being described as a "multitude of Horatio Alger stories." Emerged from humble beginnings on Chicago's Near West Side to walk the local, national, and international corridors of power. Known and respected for his personal ethics and morality. Possesses a vast collection of Abraham Lincoln memorabilia. *Photographed in his chambers in the Dirksen Federal Building.* (Chapter **25**)

James McHugh Founder and president of James McHugh Construction Co., which is one of the nation's largest and most versatile contracting firms, known for innovation. Developed new technologies for the construction of Chicago's Marina Towers, both of which still claim the title as the world's tallest concrete buildings. Was the first U.S. contractor to open an office in Moscow after the fall of communism in the Soviet Union. *Photographed across the Chicago River from Marina Towers.* (Chapter **34**)

Leo Melamed Recognized by many as the founder of financial futures. During his first term as Chairman of the Chicago Mercantile Exchange (CME), the Exchange pioneered the concept of foreign currency futures and created the International Monetary Market (IMM), the first futures market for financial instruments. Under Mr. Melamed's leadership from 1967-1991, the CME was transformed from a secondary domestic agricultural exchange to the foremost financial futures market in the world. He is currently the Chairman Emeritus of the CME and Chairman and CEO of Dellsher Investment Company Inc. *Photographed under the former Chicago Mercantile Exchange's cantilevered structure, at the corner of Jackson and Canal.* (Chapter **20**)

Richard Melman Restaurateur; raised in Chicago's Logan Square neighborhood, he is co-founder and president of *Lettuce Entertain You Enterprises, Inc.*, one of the nation's leading independent restaurant groups, which owns and licenses more than 37 restaurants in the United States and Japan. *Photographed in R.J. Grunts, wearing his lucky hat.* (Chapter **7**)

Stan Mikita Hall of Fame Blackhawks hockey player, played from 1958-1980. Holds team records for assists in a season (926), seasons played (21), games played (1,394), and 20-goal-plus seasons (14); he is second only to Bobby Hull in the total number of career goals scored. *Photographed outside of Chicago Stadium.* (Chapter **16**)

b

Anchee Min Writer, painter, photographer. In April, 1993, had a successful retrospective of her work and delivered a lecture to an overflowing audience at Shanghai's new Cultural Center. Received widespread acclaim for *Red Azalea* (Pantheon, 1994), her revealing autobiographical account of growing up in China during the height of Mao's "Cultural Revolution." *Photographed in her home on the South Side.* (Chapter **26**)

Minnie Minoso The beloved #9 for the Chicago White Sox. Rookie of the Year in 1951, led the American League for three consecutive years in stolen bases, won the Golden Glove Award in '57, '59, and '60, made seven trips to the All-Star game, and hit an impressive .304 average over his 12 year career with the Sox. Minnie is still very active with the Sox organization, and serves as the team's most popular community relations representative. *Photographed at the site of Old Comiskey Park's homeplate.* (Chapter **50**)

Clarence Page Nationally syndicated columnist and, since 1984, a member of the Chicago Tribune's editorial board. The 1989 Pulitzer Prize winner for Commentary, he is increasingly visible in the world of television journalism through appearances on *The McLaughlin Group*, the *MacNeil/Lehrer News Hour*, Black Entertainment Television's *Lead Story*, and a host of documentaries for the Public Broadcasting System. Mr. Page also does political commentary and analysis for WGN Television from "inside the Beltway," where he has worked since 1991. *Photographed in his Washington, D.C., Tribune office.* (Chapter **51**)

Walt Parazaider Co-founder of the band *Chicago*. A classically-trained musician, he studied with and was the protégé of Jerome Stowell, former E flat clarinetist in the Chicago Symphony, and is a graduate of DePaul University with a degree in orchestral clarinet performance. His Grammy Award-winning band has sold over one-hundred million records, and continues to have a worldwide influence in the incorporation of woodwinds into contemporary music. *Photographed in his home in Los Angeles.* (Chapter **5**)

Sara Paretsky Writer. Although she grew up in rural Kansas, she has called Chicago home since 1966. The city forms the backdrop of her eight novels featuring the private investigator V.I. Warshawski. On moving to Chicago she suffered the misfortune of becoming a Cubs fan. *Photographed in her Hyde Park neighborhood.* (Chapter **45**)

Ed Paschke Acclaimed artist, the leading figure of Chicago's Imagist movement. Has spent nearly three decades creating works that confront social and cultural values, often inspired by media-based imagery. In 1991, a major retrospective of his work was seen at the Art Institute of Chicago, the Dallas Museum of Art, and the Centre Pompidou, Paris. *Photographed in his Howard Street studio.* (Chapter **46**)

William Petersen A founding member of the Remains Theater Ensemble, he has appeared in numerous productions including *Once in Doubt, American Buffalo, Speed The Plow, Big Time, The Tooth of Crime,* and *Moby Dick*. At The Goodman Theater he has appeared in Tennessee Williams' *The Night of the Iguana*, and *The Time of Your Life*, on the Mainstage, and *Glengarry Glen Ross* and *Gardenia* in the studio. He has also appeared in various productions at the Stratford Festival, Steppenwolf, Wisdom Bridge, and Washington D.C.'s Kennedy Center. Film credits include *Passed Away, Hard Promises, Cousins, Young Guns II, Manhunter,* and *To Live and Die in L.A. Photographed on Kingsbury Street.* (Chapter **28**)

Liz Phair Musician; singer, songwriter. Her debut album *Exile in Guyville*, won Album of the Year honors for 1993 from *Spin, The New York Times,* and *The Village Voice; Rolling Stone* voted her Best New Female Artist. *Photographed in the "The Little Theater" at the Metro on North Clark.* (Chapter **54**)

Bill Pinkney Sailor, adventurer, author, lecturer. On August 9, 1990, embarked on his 32,000 mile, 22 month solo voyage around the globe by the most difficult, "Cape" route, in a sailboat called *Commitment*. Kept in touch with school children in Chicago and Boston via satellite, making them feel part of his epic journey. The weathered American flag he flew in every port he visited along the way is on permanent display at the DuSable Museum of African-American History. *Photographed at Belmont Harbor.* (Chapter **59**)

Barbara Proctor Chief executive officer, founder, and president of Proctor and Gardner Advertising, Inc., which has a prestigious roster of local and national clients. President Ronald Reagan, in his 1984 State of the Union address to the Nation, saluted her spirit of enterprise, referring to her as an example of one of the "heroes of the Eighties." Ms. Proctor serves on more than a dozen boards of directors, including that of the Chicago Economic Club and the DuSable Museum of African-American History, and has received hundreds of industry, civic and international recognitions. *Photographed at Soldier Field.* (Chapter **2**)

Juan Antonio Ramirez Has worked in theater, film, and television for the last 15 years. He is co-founder and artistic director of The Latino Chicago Theater Company, where he has directed over 20 stage productions. As an actor, Juan has worked at Wisdom Bridge, The Organic, and The Court, and has appeared in more than 15 films. Additionally, he is an advisor to the Graduate Program of the Time Arts Department at The School of the Art Institute. *Photographed with his son Tony, upstairs at The Latino Chicago Theater on North Damen Avenue.* (Chapter **55**)

b

Sugar Rautbord Author and socialite, fund-raiser for many charity organizations including the Alzheimer's Association. Has written many articles for magazines, including *Interview* and *Town & Country*, in addition to writing two novels, *Girls in High Places* (1987), and *Sweet Revenge* (1991). *Photographed just South of North Avenue Beach.* (Chapter **8**)

Mark Rogovin Artist and political activist. Worked in the late 1960's with the revered Mexican muralist, David Alfaro Siqueiros. Co-founded the internationally renowned Peace Museum in 1981, and currently serves on its board of directors. *Photographed with a projection of Fritz Eichenberg's The Hawk and the Dove, The Peace Museum's logo.* (Chapter **39**)

Joe Sedelmaier Known internationally for his idiosyncratic direction of humorous television commercials for such clients as Federal Express (including the Fast-Talking Man), Fiberglass (Canada), Avis (England), Mobil Oil (France), Alaska Airlines, U.S. Sprint, and Wendy's, for whom he created the famous "Where's the Beef?" commercial. He has garnered Golden Lions from the Cannes Advertising Film Festival, over 80 Clio Awards, plus eight Hall of Fame Clios, and numerous awards from the One Show, the Art Director's Club, the CA, the Hollywood IBA, and the International Festival of New York. *Photographed on a roof near his North Side home.* (Chapter **3**)

H. Gene & Joe Silverberg Clothiers, co-owners of *Bigsby & Kruthers*, the upscale men's retail store, and *The Knot Shop*, the national chain of shops specializing in ties. Together, they have become the arbiters of men's fashion in Chicago, and can rightfully claim that they clothe some of the most powerful and influential figures in the city. *Photographed beside the back door of their family's old Albany Park apartment.* (Chapter **47**)

Joyce Sloane Producer Emeritus of The Second City, has been with the company for 33 of its 34 years. Widely regarded as "Earth Mother" to a host of Chicago actors, she witnessed the rise of such Second City Alums as John Belushi, Gilda Radner, Bill Murray, and George Wendt. She has been honored for her dedicated work in the theater, and for her continuing commitments to a number of charity organizations including the Little City Foundation, Mount Sinai Medical Center, and the AIDS Foundation of Chicago. *Photographed on the stage of The Second City.* (Chapter **29**)

Richard Stern The author of 18 books, among them the novels *Golk, Other Men's Daughters, Natural Shocks,* and *A Father's Words.* His reviews, essays, and commentary have appeared in many publications here and abroad including *The New York* and *London Review(s) of Books, The New York Times, The London Times, Les Nouvelles Litteraires, Amerika (Moscow),Critical Inquiry, Hudson,* and *Partisan.* Prizes include the Medal of Merit for the Novel, an award bestowed every five years by the American Academy and Institute of Arts and Letters (past winners include Nelson Algren and Theodore Dreiser). Mr. Stern has taught at the University of Chicago since 1955. *Photographed in his University of Chicago office.* (Chapter **42**)

John Swearingen Retired as chairman of the board of directors of Standard Oil Company (Indiana), now Amoco Corporation, in 1983 after 44 years of service. He joined Standard Oil in 1939 as a chemical engineer. Widely respected in the business world, Mr. Swearingen has been awarded honorary degrees by a number of colleges and universities, and has been decorated by the governments of Egypt, Italy and Iran. He is a trustee of Carnegie-Mellon University and a former chairman and member of the board of directors of the Boys and Girls Clubs of Chicago. *Photographed at the old Union Stock Yards Gate on West Exchange Street.* (Chapter **56**)

Koko Taylor One of the world's greatest blues singer; recognized by consensus as the "Queen of the Blues." Over the course of her illustrious 30-year career, she has received nearly every award the blues world has to offer. She currently records with Alligator Records and continues to play over 200 concerts a year. *Photographed in the basement dressing room at the Cubby Bear Lounge.* (Chapter **27**)

Studs Terkel Author and, for 35 years, host of a syndicated radio show on WFMT, heard throughout the country. Most widely known for his collections of oral histories, including *Division Street: America, Working, The Great Divide, Race,* and *The Good War,* for which he won the Pulitzer Prize. *Photographed at the Border Line Tap at North and Damen Avenues.* (Chapter **60**)

Jim Thompson Four-term former Republican governor of Illinois, presently the chairman of the board of Winston & Strawn, one of Chicago's oldest and most prestigious law firms. Was instrumental in building the new Comiskey Park and keeping the White Sox at home on the South Side of Chicago. *Photographed in his seat at Comiskey Park.* (Chapter **37**)

George Wendt Comedic actor, *Second City* Alumnus; gained enormous popularity for his portrayal of "Norm" on television's *Cheers,* and as one of the ultimate Chicago Bears fans on *Saturday Night Live. Photographed on the North Side of Chicago.* (Chapter **23**)

Oprah Winfrey Host of one of the most popular television talk shows. Made her acting debut in the 1985 film, *The Color Purple,* which won her an Academy Award nomination for best supporting actress. Owns and heads the television and film production company, Harpo Studios, Inc., in the West Loop. *Photographed behind the stage of the Oprah show.* (Chapter **24**)

C

ACKNOWLEDGMENTS

Special Thanks

We would like to express our thanks to those who,
in many different ways, helped make this book possible:

Kathy Roderick, Gerry Weitz, Chris Metzler, Helane Hulbert, Burt Constable,
Lana Morgan, Patty McHugh, Harriet Voyt, Janet Miller, Ri Fournier, Robin Beamon,
Beth McNeill, Susan Frank, Terri Tomcisin, Joe Marchetti, Karen Frantz, Beryl Zitch,
John Madigan, Dr. Milton Brown, Terri Hemmert, Robert Catania, Johnny "Red" Kerr,
Susan Bergholz, Larry Viskochil, Edward Maldonado, Michael Carruth, Patty Roderick,
Michael Mulqueen, Bonnie Swearingen, Ina Pinkney, Ben Woodworth, Danny Newman,
Nora Kinnally, Carol Iwata, Maureen Frazell, Leah Berg, Melanie Neal, Mugs Magee,
William Rickman, Bill Kurtis, Henry Tabor, John Wasylic, Calvin Jones, Jeff Makos,
Fr. Ken Velo, Liz Madej, Victor Skrebneski, Richard Wentworth, Laura Parazaider,
Brenda Bullara, Lavonia Perryman, Mary Lee Montague, John Brooks, Peter Strain,
Bill Zbaren, Susan Mathieson, Scott Cameron, Martha Melman, Peter Shea,
Mary McCarthy, David Furnish, Lydia Davis Eady, Denis O'Hare,
Tom Leinfelder, Sarah Chalfant, Bob Driscoll, Antony McShane,
Eileen Younglove, John Kiker, Rita Scully, Julia Ryan and
everyone at Design Kitchen Inc.

Special thanks to:

JOHN CALLAWAY, TOM PECHOUS & RICK MARMENT

In addition, we would like to thank the following companies
for their generous help and support:

✈ UNITED AIRLINES

EASTMAN KODAK COMPANY

HENDERSON TYPOGRAPHY

NOTES:

All stories, excluding Studs Terkel's, *Chicago*, were originally written, or orally
narrated to Tom Maday and Sam Landers, for publication in *Great Chicago Stories*.
All photography was produced exclusively for *Great Chicago Stories*.

Sugar Rautbord's photo in chapter 8 includes a life-sized cardboard cut-out
of a photo reproduction of Michael Jordan. Michael Jordan does not appear
in person in this photograph.

A complete set of *Great Chicago Stories* photographic prints is part of the
Chicago Historical Society's permanent collection.

TOM MADAY & SAM LANDERS

ABOUT THE AUTHORS

Tom Maday is a photographer who shoots commercial and editorial work. Since opening a studio in 1986, his black & white and color portraits have appeared in Interview, Vogue, Rolling Stone, Esquire, Elle, Vibe, Outside, US, Men's Journal, Spin and Entertainment Weekly. Tom lives and works in the West Town neighborhood.

Sam Landers is a graphic designer and principal of Design Kitchen Inc., a graphic and package design company. His work has been recognized both nationally and internationally in publications such as Graphis, Print and Communication Arts. Sam has traveled and lived extensively abroad, but has made Chicago his home since 1983. He lives in the Old Irving Park neighborhood.

COLOPHON

The first edition of *Great Chicago Stories* is limited to 7,500 casebound copies printed on Diapaque uncoated paper, with 67 photographs reproduced as 300-line-screen tritones. Cover, text and jacket composed on Quark XPress 3.3 and Adobe Illustrator. Typeset with Sabon and Futura fonts from the Adobe Type Library. All photographs exposed on Kodak T-Max films; prints for reproduction made on Kodak Polyfiber F-surface paper and on G-surface paper for exhibition. Separations, printing and binding by Nissha Printing Co., Japan.